HOW TO WIN GRANTS

101 WINNING STRATEGIES

ALAN SILVER

ALLWORTH PRESS
NEW YORK

Allworth Press books may be purchased in bulk at special discounts for sales promotion, corporate gifts, fund-raising, or educational purposes. Special editions can also be created to specifications. For details, contact the Special Sales Department, Allworth Press, 307 West 36th Street, 11th Floor, New York, NY 10018 or info@skyhorsepublishing.com.

15   14   13   12   11   5   4   3   2   1

Published by Allworth Press
An imprint of Skyhorse Publishing
307 West 36th Street, 11th Floor, New York, NY 10018.

Allworth Press® is a registered trademark of Skyhorse Publishing, Inc.®, a Delaware corporation.

www.allworth.com

ISBN: 978-1-58115-905-9

Library of Congress Cataloging-in-Publication Data

Silver, Alan, 1949–
How to win grants : 101 winning strategies / Alan Silver.
    p. cm.
ISBN 978-1-58115-905-9 (pbk. : alk. paper)
1. Fundraising. 2. Subsidies. 3. Research grants.
4. Nonprofit organizations–Finance. I. Title.
HG177.S55 2012
658.15'224–dc23   2011048727

Printed in the United States of America

In loving memory of my parents
Victor Simon Silver and Helen Miller Silver

CONTENTS

Acknowledgments   xi

Introduction   xiii

SECTION ONE: PREPARE

1. The Basis for All Successful Grantseeking   **3**

2. Focus on "Grant Winning," Not on "Grant Writing"   **4**

3. See Grants for What They Are   **5**

4. The Grantseeker's Sweet Spot   **6**

5. Begin with the Intended Results in Mind   **8**

6. Begin Within: Assess Yourself   **9**

7. Begin Within: Assess Your Agency   **10**

8. Assess Risk: *"What's the Worst That Could Happen?"*   **12**

9. Assign Responsibility for Grants Development   **13**

10. Get Buy-In from the Boss   **14**

11. Get Your Board on Board   **15**

12. Start Early   **16**

13. Climb the Grantseeker's Learning Curve More Quickly   **17**

14. Stock—and Read—a Grants Bookshelf   **18**

15. Know When to Cut to the Chase   **20**

16. Maintain a Boilerplate File   **20**

17. Involve Experts Early and Often   **23**

18. The No-Cost Site Visit You've Got to Make   **25**

19. Prepare a Grants Development Plan   **26**

20. Avoid These Seven Deadly Grantseeking Sins   **28**

21. Get a Copy of a Funded Grant   **30**

22. Analyze Abstracts of Previously Funded Projects   **31**

23. Oink, Oink: The Art of the Earmark   **32**

24. Eschew Oft-Advertised Miracle Results   **34**

25. Get Someone Else to Get the Grant for You—For Free   **35**

26. Get Someone Else to Get the Grant for You—For a Fee   **36**

27. Get Someone Else to Get the Grant for You—For a
    Piece of the Action   **39**

28. Get Someone Else to Do the Parts You Loathe   **40**

29. On the Naming of Grant Projects   **41**

30. Plan and Prosper   **42**

31. Activate a Project Design Team   **43**

32. Project Design: Describe the Problem   **45**

33. Project Design: Describe the Solution   **47**

34. Project Design: Consider the Alternatives   **49**

35. Project Design: Replicate a Successful Project   **51**

36. Project Design: To See With New Eyes,
    Make a "Sight" Visit   **52**

37. Project Design: Consider Collaboration   **55**

38. Project Design: Plan for Impediments   **57**

39. Project Design: Work Plan   **59**

40. Project Design: Budgeting   **60**

41. Project Design: Matchmaking   **61**

42. Project Design: Sustainability   **62**

43. Project Design: Evaluation   **64**

44. Project Design: Dissemination   **66**

45. Project Design: Finish the Plan Now   **68**

46. Pilot Test Your Project   **69**

47. Overview of the Total Grant Funding Market   **69**

48. Funding Research: Independent Private Foundations   **71**

49. Funding Research: Company-Sponsored Foundations   **72**

50. Funding Research: Corporate Giving Programs   **73**

51. Funding Research: Community Foundations   **74**

52. Funding Research: Local Funding   **75**

53. Funding Research: State Funding   **76**

54. Funding Research: Federal Funding   **77**

55. Funding Research: If You Want the Scoop,
    Get in the Loop   **80**

56. Funding Research: Dialing for Dollars   **81**

57. Design the Project to Fit the Funding Criteria   **82**

58. Attend a Free Grant Opportunities Workshop   **83**

SECTION TWO: PERSUADE

59. Five Key Questions to Ask About Every
Grant Opportunity   **87**

60. Read the Instructions   **89**

61. Get Clarification   **90**

62. Keep on Track with a Tracking Tool   **91**

63. The One-Pager   **92**

64. Master the Letter of Inquiry   **94**

65. The Proposal and Its Parts   **95**

66. Writing the Abstract   **96**

67. Budgeting: Not a Dollar More, Not a Dollar Less,
Than You Need   **97**

68. Show How Your Project Achieves Others' Goals   **98**

69. When You Pass the Point of No Return,
Don't Turn Back!   **99**

70. To Be Believed, Be Specific   **102**

71. The Most Basic Form of Human Life: The "Sell"   **103**

72. Write Now, Edit Later   **104**

73. Getting Beyond Writer's Block — **105**

74. Compelling Case Studies — **107**

75. Answer the Funder's Questions — **107**

76. Set the Hook — **108**

77. The Point, and How to Get to It — **109**

78. "The Perfect is the Enemy of the Good" — **110**

79. How to Edit Your Proposal — **111**

80. Get an Earful: Read Your Draft Aloud — **112**

81. Superlatives Arouse Suspicion — **113**

82. Go Light on the Lingo — **114**

83. Give Your Proposal Curb Appeal — **115**

84. Be Merciful to Reviewers — **116**

85. Offer a Good Buy — **117**

86. Gather Evidence of Support and Commitment — **118**

87. Button-Up Checklist — **120**

88. Finish the Darn Thing and Submit It — **122**

89. Multiple Submissions — **122**

90. Hosting the Funder's Site Visit — **124**

91. If at First You Don't Succeed . . . Apply, Apply Again — **125**

SECTION THREE: PERFORM

92. Get Together at the Get-Go   **129**

93. Do, Document, Report . . . and Flourish   **130**

94. Automate the Grantseeking and Grants
Management Process   **133**

95. Married . . . with Funders   **133**

96. Spend the Money   **134**

97. Become a Grant Reviewer   **136**

98. Toot Your Own Horn (or Hire a Tooter)   **137**

99. Keep Track of Your Results   **138**

100. Winning from Losing   **139**

101. How to Keep Winning Grants   **140**

Index   143

ACKNOWLEDGEMENTS

My experience with grants dates to 1977, when I was hired to develop and manage a nonprofit health care program in rural North Carolina. There, I had the opportunity to learn from experience, including the valuable experience of failure, what works and what doesn't work when it comes to grantseeking. I also had the good fortune to befriend the late Will Harper, a West Virginian who knew how to win grants. I will never forget the evening Will showed up at my office, bottle of bourbon in hand, to help me put together my first grant request. Of course, we didn't crack the seal on the bourbon until the grant request was done.

I am thankful to the clients who have employed me to help them win grants over the last three decades. Their confidence has helped me brave with them the risk of failure, even though for the most part we have enjoyed success. This success, which has financed tens of millions of dollars worth of grant-funded projects to promote better health and safety, is the raw material out of which this book was built.

I appreciate the advice and encouragement of Tad Crawford and Delia Casa at Skyhorse Publishing. I especially want to thank Savannah writer Susan B. Johnson for reading and copyediting the manuscript and for her many helpful suggestions. Any remaining errors or omissions in the text are all mine.

My deepest gratitude goes to my darling wife, Patricia. She has listened to my grantseeking tales of wonder and woe, read and helped me improve upon many and diverse grant requests, and observed firsthand my at times deadline-defying grantseeking behavior. And she has had the good sense and grace to comment productively, patiently, lovingly.

INTRODUCTION

Every year, nonprofit organizations win billions of dollars in grants. How do they do it? What's more important, how can *you* do it? This book shows you how, with a simple, three-stage approach to winning grants:

Stage One: Prepare (Strategies #1-58) readies you to seek grants by showing you how to assess and improve your personal and agency positioning for grants, plan competitive projects, and identify the best sources of grant funding. This section also dispels several widespread myths about grantseeking and identifies unproductive grantseeking behaviors to avoid. Nearly two-thirds of the 101 strategies involve preparing to compete, homage to the "6P" truth that "Proper prior planning prevents poor performance."

Stage Two: Persuade (Strategies #59-91) shows you how to convince private and public funders that your project merits funding. You'll see how writing the grant application becomes a matter of adapting your already drafted project plan to the specific needs of each potential funder. You'll learn how to engage the funder's attention and make the most compelling case for your project.

Stage Three: Perform (Strategies #92-101) will help you see effective ways to continue to attract grant funding over the long-term.

How to Win Grants is as short as I could write it. My aim is to give you a concise, lively guide that you can digest in one sitting and return to for ideas as you go about your grantseeking. I also hope this book contributes to better grant applications and, by extension, more effective grant-funded projects.

YOU CAN TELL *THIS* BOOK BY ITS COVER

This is a book about "how to win grants"—not just about how to write grant applications, because persuasive writing skills are only a part of successful grantseeking. If you grasp the significance of the last sentence and can put it to use, you will have gotten your money's worth from this book. In short, you don't need to write like William Shakespeare (and you'd better not!) to win grants. You just need to adapt and develop three skills you already possess: the ability to plan, the ability to convince others that your plan is worth funding, and the ability to manage the grants you win so as to achieve successful results.

WHAT YOU WON'T FIND IN THIS BOOK

You won't find the following in this book:

- Information on how to incorporate your agency or to obtain federal tax-exempt status
- Information on grantseeking for individuals (for example, scholarships) or businesses (for example, money to start a business)

- Information on fundraising, much of which is focused on asking wealthy individuals to part with cash for good causes
- Cookbook-type recipes or so-called magic words that purport to guarantee funding
- Samples of abstracts, narratives, budgets and other portions of funded grant projects; as noted in the text, there are ample free or reasonably priced sources for such materials
- Page after page of website listings of potential funding sources (As you'll see, you need to master a few key databases and do your own research.)

I HOPE YOU'LL READ OTHER BOOKS ON THIS SUBJECT

Over the years, I've found many worthwhile books and much excellent Internet content that explains the grantseeking process. Some of this material is interesting, but some of it is excruciatingly detailed and a tough slog. At the opposite end of the spectrum, there is also a fair amount of disinformation for sale that can dent your wallet without improving your grant-winning prospects. I hope you will avoid cheesy Internet scams that offer computer disks and outdated print materials. You can learn about alternative approaches to grantseeking from the kinds of sources shown in the text, specifically in Strategy # 14.

A FEW WORDS ON TERMINOLOGY

Terms frequently and inconsistently used in the world of grantseeking and grants management can confuse you if you are unfamiliar with them and if you let them. For example, some funders use the terms "goal" and "objective" as if they mean the same thing (as you will see, they do not). There are not enough academic bones in my body to devise, and ask you to sit through, a discussion of the meaning of oft-used grantseeking terms. Instead, if you will provisionally accept at times inconsistent grantseeking terminology, you will over time figure out with increasing precision what each funder means. I myself have used three terms for convenience and brevity that I would like to explain. By "funder," I mean any entity, public or private, that makes grants. By "agency," I mean a tax-exempt entity that seeks grants. By "target population," I mean the people or thing (such as the environment) your grant seeks to benefit.

"FREE MONEY" OR "DISCOUNT DOLLARS"?

Contrary to what you may have heard, grants are not "free money." First, applying for grants isn't "free"—just see what happens to your "free time" when you write a grant application. And when you win a grant, the real work begins. If grants were free, you could do whatever you pleased with the money. But your funding request is your firm offer to undertake specific, socially useful activities with the grant funds. The consequences of doing otherwise range from having to pay back the funder to incurring hefty fines and jail time. It's best to think of a grant as a binding promise, or contract, whereby your agency agrees to do something socially useful with OPM (other people's money).

I like to think of grants as "discount dollars"—funds that buy down the cost of critically needed investments in new or improved programs, services, equipment, or facilities. Let's say your agency needs to purchase new communications equipment, but can only afford to budget 25 percent of the total system cost each year for the next four years. Given today's rapid rate of technological obsolescence, that's not an appetizing strategy. Instead, you find a technology grant with a 25 percent cash match requirement that enables you to buy the entire system this year—now that's a deep discount! Even when you factor in the work involved in writing the application and managing the grant, you've improved your communication system this year and preserved the next three years' capital funds for other needed projects.

AND A COUPLE OF CAVEATS

The prepare-persuade-perform model enables you to see the entire grantseeking and grants management process as part of a continuum. Any model, however, is an abstraction from life, and therefore a distortion. Further, any attempt to segment a continuous, iterative process in the form of three stages and 101 strategies is bound to confuse the reader seeking a cookbook approach. Know that the strategies presented herein will have varying value to you depending on your personal and agency situation. In a similar vein, the answer to the grantseeker's conundrum ("What comes first, the project or the funding?") is that either will do nicely. If you start with a good project, you can go hunting for grant support; if the funding source appears before you have a project plan, get moving on that plan!

You might also benefit from considering your grantseeking efforts in terms of where your agency is in the nonprofit life cycle (there are numerous life-cycle typologies, but they typically start with birth or infancy, and end in death or, in some cases, more hopefully, in renewal). If your agency is very young and has no grants track record, you may need to begin modestly, with small, local grants, and progress to larger requests as you demonstrate your stewardship of grant funds. Conversely, well-established agencies may find it increasingly challenging to identify and attract new sources of grant funding despite their successful grants track records.

IN SUMMARY

While writing this book, I imagined a continuum of readers, from neophytes who have never requested grant funding and don't know where to start to veteran grantseekers who are always looking for ways to improve their "win rate." I hope I have offered useful information to you, regardless of where you currently hang out along the grantseeking continuum. I think that if you use the strategies in this book along with your own good sense, you will win grants. It is that simple, although it is not that easy; it is, after all, work.

SECTION ONE

Prepare

"It is all in being ready."
JOSEPH CONRAD, LORD JIM

1

The Basis for All
Successful Grantseeking

The basis for all successful grantseeking consists of three things:

- A well-defined problem or need
- A plausible strategy to address that problem or meet that need
- A persuasively presented funding request from an eligible, qualified applicant

2

Focus on "Grant Winning," Not on "Grant Writing"

The overwhelming focus of most neophyte grant seekers is on the writing process. This is a mistake. If instead you will focus on *winning* grants, you can think backward to what it takes to win.

First, it takes a sufficiently detailed plan. If you will not skip or shortchange the design phase, you can trick yourself into doing a good deal of the writing you will need to apply for funding. That's because virtually all funders want to know the same things—who you are, what you want, why it's important, how much it will cost, why and how your project will work, and what happens to the project when the grant ends. The written answers to these kinds of questions are the basis for an effective plan.

Second, you need to find the likeliest sources of funding and the other resources you need to make the project work. This means you need to fully explore and rule out non-grant funding sources before seeking a grant for your project. Then, if grantseeking is indicated by your written plan, you adapt your plan to the needs and requirements of each funder in the form of a compelling funding request.

The goal of a successful grants development program is to win grants.

3

See Grants for What They Are

A grant is an exchange of values between two entities undertaken to pursue socially beneficial results. One entity (the grantor) pays the other (the grantee) to undertake activities as its agent.

A grant is not a gift because you can't do whatever you want with the money. Grants involve a quid pro quo: The grantor pays the grantee, and the grantee is obligated to do specific things. In some instances, however, agencies are awarded funds that they are authorized to re-grant to other agencies.

A grant is not a contract, although the nature of the exchange between grantor and grantee can be reduced to writing in contractual form.

Grants can be understood as social experiments whereby grantors provide resources with the hope of achieving results. Some grant-funded experiments can last for decades, while others represent one-time funding.

Grants can help your agency extend its programs and services to new geographic areas and new target populations, or address barriers to service that negatively impact your current service delivery (for example, by providing transportation that enables your target population to access your services).

4

The Grantseeker's Sweet Spot

Focus your grantseeking efforts on the sweet spot: where your agency's needs, the funder's needs, and the needs of your target population overlap:

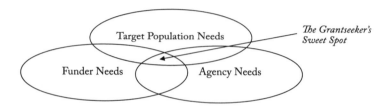

The target population's needs:

- May be better understood and documented by supplementing agency staff viewpoints and agency data with interviews and focus groups composed of the target population and other individuals and agencies that come into contact with them, and also from local, regional, and national needs assessments, reports and research
- May be better understood within the context of other environmental, economic, political, social, and cultural influences
- May change over time, to the extent that, if these needs haven't been reconsidered lately, your agency's efforts may be getting diminishing results

Your agency's needs:

- Should be closely aligned with the needs of your target population
- May include such items as staff training and facility and equipment upgrades in order to serve the target population more effectively

The funder's needs:

- Should focus on funding projects that get specific, socially beneficial results
- Are particular to each funder;
  - ○ If a public funder, these needs include wisely investing tax dollars in accordance with public laws and administrative regulations.
  - ○ If a private funder, these needs include making grants that further the funder's stated mission and goals.
- Include not making grants to agencies that don't follow through as promised. (Funders have a long institutional memory for grantees who make them look bad.)

5

Begin with the Intended Results in Mind

Grantseeking based solely on the observation that "we need the money" is reactive and doomed to fail. Know why you are seeking grants and communicate your motivations at all levels of your agency.

Grants enable you to:

1. Advance your mission and service objectives when needs exceed available resources
2. Pursue a new mission, serve a new target population or geographic area, or fund new activities
3. Diversify agency revenues so you are not overly dependent on one or a few sources of funding
4. Experiment and innovate with OPM (other people's money) when your agency lacks "risk capital"
5. Leverage planned expenditures, thereby achieving a multiplier effect and enabling you to implement more quickly

Your reasons for grantseeking should be reduced to writing in the Grants Development Plan recommended in Strategy #19.

6

Begin Within: Assess Yourself

Successful grantseeking begins with knowing who you are as a grantseeker.

Assess your readiness in terms of these major grantseeking competencies:

1. Needs Analysis: How well do you know your target population's needs and your agency's needs?
2. Planning: How thoroughly do you plan projects and programs? Can you develop clear and attainable objectives, assess likely obstacles, and estimate realistic budgets and timelines?
3. Research: How efficiently and effectively can you identify and prioritize your agency's grant funding opportunities and the key sources of potential funding for your agency and projects?
4. Salesmanship: How effectively can you make the case for your entity's needs, in writing and in person?
5. Grants Management Track Record: How many grants have you managed, and how well have you managed them? What were the results of these grants for your target population and your agency?

For areas where you find yourself lacking, develop strategies to enhance your competency with help from other people and reference material.

If you are seeking grants as part of a team, the above readiness questions can be asked and answered within the team context.

7

Begin Within: Assess Your Agency

Whether you are a veteran grantseeker or the "chief cook and bottle washer" of a fledgling nonprofit, you can benefit from assessing your agency's positioning to pursue and manage grants. Depending on the amount of time you're willing to devote to the assessment process, you can:

1. Complete the assessment as part of a comprehensive Grants Development Plan (Strategy #19) or merely as a planning exercise before you ramp up your grantseeking activities, or
2. Assess your agency's readiness for grantseeking by using the Boilerplate File (Strategy #16) as a checklist, or

3. Get insight into your agency's level of grantseeking competitiveness and develop a readiness to-do list by completing a SWOT analysis*

Strengths might include such factors as:

- Reputation and service record
- Responsiveness to changing needs
- Cost-effective service delivery and demonstrable outcomes
- Stable, qualified management and staffing, some of whom have writing and research abilities and interests

Weaknesses might include such factors as:

- Minimal grantseeking and grants management experience; low visibility with potential funders
- Insufficient staff and other resources to pursue grants
- Lack of documentation to support grantseeking (see Strategy #16, Maintain a Boilerplate File)

Opportunities might include such factors as:

- List of specific grants for which your agency is eligible
- Agencies that share your agency's target population and want to collaborate

---

*SWOT (which stands for Strengths, Weaknesses, Opportunities, and Threats) was developed in the 1960s and 1970s by Albert Humphrey, a Stanford University researcher. Numerous online SWOT resources provide detailed questions to ask under each SWOT category.

- Board and volunteer relationships with potential funders

Threats might include such factors as:

- Competition from other public or private agencies that serve the same target population
- Declining public interest in the needs your agency serves

8

Assess Risk: "What's the Worst That Could Happen?"*

What is likely to happen when you apply for grants?

1. You are likely to win sometimes and lose sometimes.
2. Your results are likely to improve over time as your skills and knowledge increase.
3. You are unlikely to exhaust all potential funding sources.

---

*This is also the title of a funny novel by Donald Westlake. To read chilling accounts of personal risk assessment under life-challenging conditions, see Dale Carnegie's *How to Stop Worrying and Start Living*. It may put your worries in perspective.

Grantseeking is neither dangerous nor risky when compared to most other activities. If you can accept the most likely negative consequence of applying for grants—failure—and learn from it, you can continue to improve your results.

9

Assign Responsibility for Grants Development

For the job of grant development to get done, someone in your agency needs to be assigned to do it, typically by the CEO. It's the same for grants management.

In a larger agency, especially one with numerous departments (a.k.a. "silos"), a grants committee can be useful, even essential.* The committee, chaired by a senior manager whose job description explicitly includes grants development and grants management, can be charged with monitoring compliance of awarded grants and assessing and pursuing new grant opportunities in the Grants Development Plan that are aligned with the agency's mission and service objectives. The committee ought to meet regularly and keep a brief written record of its activities, including its

---

*Imagine how a funder might react if approached by two people from two different departments of a large agency who seek funding for similar or competing projects.

recommendations to the CEO. In larger agencies, this committee should include staff with roles in direct service delivery, community outreach, marketing/public education, and accounting/financial management. The committee should also be responsible for annually evaluating the agency's grantseeking and grants management results, and using this evaluation to update the agency's Grants Development Plan.

10

Get Buy-In from the Boss

Your agency chief's support for the grantseeking process is essential to your success. After all, your chief will most likely need to assign responsibility for grantseeking and grants management, allocate agency resources to grant projects, approve proposals, and in many instances, obtain board of directors' approval.

Busy agency executives are routinely bombarded with staff opinions, ideas, and notions. Help your chief separate the wheat from the chaff. Refine your project idea as much as possible before you make your pitch. A one-pager or brief concept paper may be all you need to get buy-in to proceed with project planning, but be prepared to address questions about revenue and expense impacts and post-grant sustainability.

11

Get Your Board on Board

If you work for a private nonprofit agency, you have a board of directors and perhaps other advisory panels. These folks may be able to help you win grants.

With your agency chief leading the way, try the following strategies to maximize board involvement in the grantseeking process:

- Make sure your board understands your agency's need to seek grant funding and supports your grants development plan.
- Ask them who they know that can help fund your projects (examples include trustees at local foundations and company executives with authority to make corporate contributions to your project).
- Ask them to help you by attending funder site visits, "making the call" to corporate funders, and participating in other activities for which they are prepared and enthusiastic.

12

Start Early

The early bird, so the saying goes, gets the worm (the early worm is less fortunate). And so it goes with grantseeking: If you start early, you are more likely to win.

Many publicly funded grants at the local, state, and federal levels don't change much from year to year. So be aware of the governmental unit's annual budget cycle, get a copy of the prior year's guidelines, and begin designing and developing your project. If the underlying legislation that authorized the grant program hasn't changed and funds have been appropriated, the guidelines for the upcoming grant cycle may not change much. Even if the guidelines change, you'll have begun working through all the time-consuming issues that must be resolved before you're ready to write the application.

While some private funders change their funding priorities often, others have funding priorities that endure from year to year. Funders who like your project may simply not have enough money to fund it—this year. Why not cultivate the opportunity to get in their budget for the coming year?

A long-range view of the grantseeking process is attuned to the reality that many needs chase limited resources. Just as "chance favors the prepared mind," you will have a plan ready so that when funding is announced, you can tailor your plan to fit the funding.

13

Climb the Grantseeker's Learning Curve More Quickly

These suggestions are for the first-time or inexperienced grantseeker:

- Read several books to get different perspectives on grantseeking (see Strategy #14). Find out if there are books on grantseeking targeted to your area of interest and read these for specific information.
- Take a course, seminar, or workshop on grant writing offered by your community college, four-year college or university, the Foundation Center, or other reputable organization or grants consultant.
- Subscribe to and read periodicals focused on the non-profit world, philanthropy, and grants, such as the *Nonprofit Times* and the *Journal of Philanthropy*. Some cities and many states now have nonprofit associations that publish useful newsletters.
- Get on email notification lists sponsored by grants consultants, foundations, and state and federal governments.

14

Stock—and Read—a Grants Bookshelf

Here are a few suggestions of books and periodicals to keep up with trends and changes in trends in the nonprofit world that directly impact grantseeking and grants management:

- For detailed treatments of grantseeking and grant writing, see such books as Beverly A. Browning's *Grant Writing for Dummies*, and the following three books by Cheryl Carter New and James Aaron Quick: *How to Write a Grant Proposal; Grantseeker's Toolkit: A Comprehensive Guide to Finding Funding;* and *Grant Winner's Toolkit: Project Management and Evaluation.*
- Another good source of grant development guidance is Lynn E. Miner and Jeremy T. Miner's *Proposal Planning and Writing, 4th Edition.* Also from these writers, see *Models of Proposal Planning and Writing*, which provides examples of funded proposals.
- *The Foundation Center's Guide to Proposal Writing*, by Jane C. Geever, now in its fifth edition, is a standard reference that thoroughly addresses all aspects of proposal development.
- To understand how foundations operate, read Mark Dowie's *American Foundations, An Investigative History.* Another good source is Joel J. Orosz's *The Insider's Guide to Grantmaking: How Foundations Find, Fund, and Manage Effective Programs.*

- For a good annual update on charitable giving trends, read *Giving USA*, a publication of the Giving USA Foundation™, researched and written by the Center on Philanthropy at Indiana University.
- There are numerous free online guides to proposal writing, including the Community Tool Box (*www. cbt.ku.edu*) and "Writing Grants" at the Catalog of Federal Domestic Assistance (*www.cfda.gov*).
- Books on the writing process can help you too. One of my favorites is Henriette Ann Klauser's *Writing on Both Sides of the Brain*. It abounds with practical ideas on outlining, visualization, dealing with procrastination, and other writing issues. You can get pointers on editing your writing from Barry Tarshis's *How to be Your Own Best Editor: The Toolkit for Everyone Who Writes*.

If you are on a tight budget, order books on interlibrary loan through your local library, or visit a Foundation Center Cooperating Collection near you (see *www.foundationcenter .org* for a list of libraries and locations).

In general, avoid books composed primarily of lists of grant funding sources; this information is best accessed online.

15

Know When to Cut to the Chase

If you are accustomed to thinking that someone else always has a better answer to a problem than you do, or that you always need consensus to proceed with a project, or that you must read one more book or attend one more seminar before you move ahead with your project—you, my friend, may be what is known as a procrastinating perfectionist.

You do not need any specific training, licensure, or certification to win grants. You need a constellation of competencies—planning, persuasion, and performance—that you can best develop with practice.

Books, seminars, workshops, and the like are fine, but don't let them put off your day of reckoning. Improve your chances to win grants by preparing well and then competing for grants: there is simply no better teacher than asking for the money.

16

Maintain a Boilerplate File

You can save time and effort with each successive grant application by developing hard-copy and electronic files with key agency information. When you are ready to apply for funding, you will have most of the "boilerplate" funders ask for ready to insert into your applications with minor revisions. Here is an outline of the kinds of information you will want to have handy:

- Documentation of agency legal status (for private, nonprofit agencies: state charter, Internal Revenue Service tax-exemption letter, articles of incorporation, bylaws, and annual tax filings; for public agencies: the statutory basis for your agency's existence)
- Agency mission, vision, and values
- Description of services, programs, staffing, fees, eligibility, or admissions criteria
- Descriptive information on your geographic service area and target population (including state, regional, national comparisons)
- What makes your agency special (examples include unique mission, quality, and cost metrics, board/volunteers/staff)
- Board of directors table with names, addresses, phone/fax/email, race/gender/age, affiliations
- Volunteers: numbers, roles, hours, and the aggregate annual economic value of the time they contribute
- Key management and staff (biographical sketches/resumes/CVs showing specialized skills/qualifications)
- Summary statistics/utilization data (clients served/year, etc.)

- Key performance indicators and trends (cost per client or per encounter, number of clients served per year, comparison to industry standards)
- Brief agency history
- Accreditation, awards/achievements, memberships, and coalition and partnership relationships
- Facility or program licensure and certifications, including qualifications of key personnel
- Facilities, locations, days, and hours of service
- Facility floor plans
- Agency and program brochures or flyers
- Organizational chart
- Service area map
- Annual work plan and budget
- Needs assessments
- Strategic or long-range plan
- Annual report
- List of websites with relevant demographic, statistical reference, and needs assessment information
- Technology plan
- Graphic or flow chart of how clients access agency services
- One-page annual revenue and expense summary with category percentages, including salaries and fringe benefits
- Documentation of indirect cost rate, if you have one
- Internal and independent evaluations of services and programs
- Client satisfaction survey methods and results
- Audited financial statements (three years)

- Grants track record (see Strategy # 99)
- Lists of relevant contracts and memoranda of understanding or agreement
- Media coverage and testimonials
- Annual calendar of agency events

17

Involve Experts Early and Often

You can improve your chances of being funded and executing a successful project if you involve people with relevant expertise in the project design process. These people, sometimes called SMEs (subject matter experts), can come from inside and outside your agency.

- If it's a human services project, ask the intended target population what they think. How? You can use phone and written surveys, focus groups, one-on-one interviews, brainstorming sessions, or town hall meetings. Pick the method or methods easiest for your target population. Be sure to document the results.
- If it's an information technology project, involve computer geeks. None on staff? Get help from local colleges or university information technology

departments, or vendors or tech companies with staff knowledgeable about proven and emerging technologies.

- If it's a health care project, involve clinicians—not only those at your agency, but also those whose opinions can make or break the project in the medical community.
- If it's a construction or renovation project, board members may have valuable expertise, and architects and construction companies may give you free advice in the hopes you will hire them.

When it comes to experts, you can get useful design ideas in three ways:

- One-on-one interviews, which often elicit more information than group sessions, especially from shy people with great ideas. Generally, face-to-face meetings are more informative than phone interviews or email queries. Phone and email are good for follow-up questions and feedback on draft project designs, but they don't encourage extended thinking and comment focused on your project.
- Group sessions, which can run the gamut from brainstorming to a structured, facilitated planning process
- Print materials and online books, articles, and blogs focused on the subject matter. Chances are someone has tried a project like yours and can offer good advice about how to proceed for best results.

18

The No-Cost Site Visit You've Got to Make

When you've identified potential funders for your project, visit their websites to read all about them. While small, private foundations may not have a website, you can still Google them to see what's been said by or about them.

Before you phone a funder to discuss a project, you should learn as much as is publicly known about the funder, including:

- Mission and current funding priorities
- Whether they fund agencies like yours
- How much grant money they have available
- Current grant opportunities, guidelines, timelines
- Funding patterns—grantee names, amounts, abstracts of funded projects, percentage of applicants funded
- Whether they encourage potential applicants to call with questions or discuss proposed projects, and, if so, whom you can call
- Downloadable publications that will help you in your planning

Revisit relevant websites often, put them on your favorites list, and register for email notification of new funding opportunities if this feature is available.

19

Prepare a Grants Development Plan

One of the most useful strategies you can employ to diversify your agency revenues is to prepare a grants development plan. The plan should identify services, program and capital needs, public and private funding sources, and grants management requirements (how funding will impact your agency's day-to-day work). As with other planning efforts, the process of developing the plan can be as important as, or more important than, the final plan. Nevertheless, it's crucial that you complete a written plan document: That's what you will use to manage your grantseeking and measure your results.

Agency management should assign responsibility and timelines for preparing, executing, and updating the plan. You will want to integrate the grants development plan with your overall agency strategic and annual operating plans. What might be included in a grants development plan? Here's a suggested outline:

Title Page: Agency Name, Grants Development Plan, Timeframe, Date Completed

Table of Contents (paginated for quick reference)

Executive Summary (a one-page overview for CEO and board-level leadership)

I. Introduction
  A. Purpose (presumably to diversify revenues and improve grantseeking and grants management results; reduce your reasons to writing so you can evaluate later)

B. Scope (how the plan relates to your agency's mission)

C. Methods (the processes and information sources you used to prepare the plan, including review of agency documents, interviews with stakeholders and funding agencies, site visits to other agencies and programs, research in public and proprietary databases)

II. Current Situation, Operating Environment and Trends

A. Agency Grants Experience (your agency grants track record, and SWOT—strengths, weaknesses, opportunities, and threats) as it relates to grantseeking

B. Agency Metrics (comparison of your agency's operations to other local, regional, and national indices)

C. Agency Operating Environment and Trends (what is going on locally, regionally, nationally, internationally; industry best practices)

III. Goals, Objectives, and Strategies

A. How the Plan Will Be Managed (who is responsible for execution)

B. Management Matrix (This section, the heart of the plan, objectifies your agency capital and program funding needs; it details the "who, what, when, why, and how" for executing the plan, organized in a table with goals, objectives, strategies, three-year timelines, responsible persons, and expected results/measurement.)

C. Grants Opportunities (a three-year projection with detail on where you think your grants will come from, prioritized in descending order of importance)

Appendices

   A. Planning Process Participants (who was involved in developing the plan, including agency staff, community leaders, funding agency contacts, and others)

   B. Selected References (relevant local, regional, and national plans, journal articles, news articles on industry trends, and the like)

   C. Year 1 Grants Opportunities At-A-Glance (one-pager that summarizes the likely funding sources for each Year 1 objective, funding program titles, working title for your projects, grant and match estimates, and total budget)

20

Avoid These Seven Deadly Grantseeking Sins

Instantly improve your grant funding chances by avoiding these no-no's:

1. Don't ask for money from people who will never give it to you. If the Dinkey-Doo Foundation says they don't fund agencies outside the Gotham City

metro area and you are based in rural Burgdorf, don't waste your time. If you need a construction grant and Big Bux Foundation funds only services and programs, don't bother.

2. Don't shotgun cookie-cutter proposals to long lists of funders. It takes time and patience to customize your request for each funder, but it pays off in proposals targeted to *their* funding priorities.

3. Don't contact funders until you have learned about their funding priorities, types of projects and grantees, geographic preferences, and all the other things you can find out in a few minutes by reading their website or consulting the Foundation Center database.

4. Don't ask for funding before you know exactly what you need. It is fine to discuss a project in general terms at an early stage with a funding agency contact, but before you ask for money, you must thoroughly plan the project and anticipate the funder's questions.

5. Don't submit a grant proposal without having another person read it for meaning, content, and style. Even if you were marooned on a desert island, you could at least read your proposal aloud and listen to yourself.

6. Don't talk too much about your project and write too little about it.

7. Don't give up too soon. If you have a good idea and you refine its presentation, it's increasingly likely someone will fund it—maybe even the funder who originally rejected your proposal.

21

Get a Copy of a Funded Grant

One way you can gain confidence in your ability to develop a grant project is to get copies of successful (funded) grant proposals and study them. If you've been baffled or timid about grantseeking, or just curious about what a grant application looks like—especially those thick federal applications—you will see that there's no magic to a funded application, just a lot of hard work.

How do you get a copy of a funded grant proposal? Sources include:

- Colleagues at other agencies, especially where there is no competition in serving the same geographic area or target population, and when your agencies seek funds from different funding sources
- Books on grantseeking, such as Jeremy T. Miner and Lynn E. Miner's *Models of Proposal Planning and Writing*
- Websites that offer grant applications for sale, typically in CD format. For example, the Grantsmanship Center, *www.tgci.com*, has hundreds of funded applications in CD format in a searchable database.

For federal grants, you should be aware of the Freedom of Information Act (FOIA), a law that gives citizens the right to gain access to federal agency documents and other records. Exemptions, exclusions, and fees may apply, and each federal agency has its own FOIA website with guidelines on how to submit a request; a master list is at *www.justice.gov/oip/foiacontacts.htm*. State laws, which are usually called Open Records acts, govern access to state grant applications.

Reading funded grant applications is likely to give you some good ideas about how to organize and present your project, but copying others' grant proposals is unethical, unlikely to get you funded, and guaranteed to send you straight to hell when you die.

22

Analyze Abstracts of Previously Funded Projects

One of the quickest, easiest ways to get a feel for funders' priorities is to read and analyze abstracts of similar, previously funded projects, usually accessed via foundation or government websites. Some sites may show you only a two or three sentence summary of the project, while others reproduce the entire abstract as written by the applicant.

Use the abstracts to discern the following kinds of information:

- Past funding patterns
- Changes in funding patterns
- The scope and scale of funded projects

- Grantee entity status
- Geographic locations funded
- Project titles

In some cases, you can estimate project cost-effectiveness or unit costs by dividing the budget by the units of service or numbers of persons to be served. If several similar projects are profiled, you might be able to determine a range of costs per unit of service acceptable to the funder.

23

Oink, Oink: The Art of the Earmark

In keeping with the central thesis of this book—that you will get better results by focusing on *winning* grants rather than *writing* grants—this strategy shows you how to seek project funding via state or federal earmarks.

Earmarks (also called "pork barrel funding," "appropriations," "special appropriations," or "directed appropriations") are secured with the help of your local, state, or federal elected officials. Earmarks are controversial because they are awarded primarily based on political influence and because some projects appear to be a big waste of taxpayers' money.

How do you do it?

- Write up a one-pager that summarizes your project and explains who you are, what you need, why the project merits funding, and who supports it.
- Schedule a meeting with your representative and make your request. Be prepared to explain why you are not seeking this funding from another source. Sometimes you will be asked to coordinate your request through a legislative aide; you might also be asked to complete a narrative outline.
- Follow up from time to time to check on the status of your request. It may be necessary for you to resubmit your request to coincide with subsequent legislative sessions due to a backlog of unfunded requests.

To win:

- Show how your project benefits large numbers of voters (and while you are at it, come up with a compelling but realistic number).
- Time your request in sync with the state or federal budget process.
- Focus on one-time projects; legislators do not want to see you back every year for continuing programmatic budget support.

Earmarks can be extraordinarily cost-effective in terms of the time and effort required to produce results. Here's a true story: While managing a nonprofit agency, I organized a breakfast for our state legislative delegation. Over eggs, bacon, biscuits, and grits, our board and staff briefly outlined our agency services and contribution to the community, then noted our funding needs. Our elected officials responded weeks later with numerous five- and ten-thousand dollar appropriations earmarked for our agency. Incidentally, if you use the "eggs and begs" approach, interaction between your stakeholders and legislators is essential (we assigned seating so our board and staff were sprinkled among the legislators).

24

Eschew* Oft-Advertised Miracle Results

You can save gobs of time, effort, money, and disappointment by ignoring the self-proclaimed experts who purport to sell sure-fire grant-getting systems. To hear the TV and Web-based pitchmen tell it, all you've got to do is buy their software, fill-in-the-blanks, and hit "enter" to win grants.

There is ample, high-quality grantseeking advice on the Internet, much of it free, some of it provided by respected funding information sources that constantly update their databases and provide reasonably priced subscription access. What you will find via these sources is more accurate and up-to-date than the hucksters' offerings, and less likely to mislead you about where to find funding for your agency.

---

*If you want to lose weight, eschew food.

You simply cannot shortcut the work involved in planning a project, finding the funding sources for which your agency is eligible and well-positioned to win, and crafting proposals targeted to each of these funding sources.

25

Get Someone Else to Get the Grant for You—For Free*

If you want to get free grantseeking help, you've got to be creative—and patient. Here are a few possibilities:

- A local college or university, where students need real-world experience—backed up by their professor. Consider their semester or quarter scheduling and plan ahead.
- Economic development agencies, councils of governments, and similar tax-supported agencies know where the funding is and how to get it. They may help you make your case with local and regional data.
- Companies that sell the products and services you want to buy with grant funding often know about

---

*This strategy and the next three strategies describe alternative ways to organizing the work of grantseeking. Consider them within the context of your unique set of personal and agency circumstances.

funding sources, and some even employ staff who can help you. They may have a list of likely funding sources and copies of previously funded projects. Use their written material with care; it is written from a sales perspective that will be evident to grant reviewers unless integrated stylistically with the rest of your funding proposal.

Do as much as you can to plan the project before you ask for help. In other words, narrow the scope of work with which you need outside assistance. When you negotiate the arrangement for free help, put it in writing. Make it clear you'll be the final judge of whether the grant proposal has enough merit to be submitted. And finally, show your appreciation for the help you get: for example, via thank you letter, thank you lunch, and recognition in agency newsletters and local newspapers.

26

Get Someone Else to Get the Grant for You—For a Fee

If you can't or won't write the grant request yourself, and you can't get someone to do it for free, or for a piece of the action, you can pay a grants consultant (typically called a grant writer) to do it for you.

Any grants consultant worth his or her salt is as busy as he or she wants to be, so you may have to plan well ahead of your needs.

How do you find a grants consultant? Ask around, because word-of-mouth reputation can make or break a grants consultant. Start by calling your colleagues, some of whom may use grants consultants. Call local organizations, such as your United Way headquarters, and regional and state associations; many of them may keep lists of consultants' names.

Like other kinds of consulting, grants consulting is an easy field to enter: All you need to get started is a phone, a mouth, and moxie. Expect to devote a couple of hours of work to phoning nonprofit colleagues for names and lining up candidates to interview.

Here are some questions to ask the grants consultant:

- What do you know about our agency, our services, and our operating environment?
- Given the needs we've described, how would you approach this project?
- How long have you been in this business? Why are you in this business? What did you do before you were a grants consultant?
- How would you work with us? Do you disappear with the signed contract and reappear the day before the deadline with a finished product? Do we get to review and approve a draft well ahead of the deadline?
- What funding research capabilities do you have? How do you find funding sources?
- What kind of success rate do you have overall and with this kind of proposal?

- What kind of operational experience do you have? (It is one thing to forecast budgets, another to live under them.)
- How do you charge for your services? (Let's see your contract proposal.)

You should ask for writing samples and references. Give the consultant every opportunity to help you by being clear on the scope of work—does the consultant merely edit a draft proposal, coach your staff on grantseeking, or develop the project from A to Z?

Remember, rarely can you pay the consultant out of the grant you hope to win, although occasionally some funders may pay seed money for you to engage a grants consultant to help you apply for larger grants.

Even if you use a grants consultant, you will still have to do a substantial amount of work, especially if this is the first project the consultant has worked on for you. Be prepared to provide lots of oversight, since your agency—not the consultant—must perform on the promises you make to the grant funder.

27

Get Someone Else to Get the Grant for You—For a Piece of the Action

If you lack the wherewithal to develop your own funding applications and can't pay for a grants consultant or find free help, you may still be able to access grant funding. Consider these bootstrap strategies:

- Partner with a freelance writer, evaluator, consultant or temporarily-out-of-work professional. In this scenario, your appropriately qualified helper writes the application for you with the prospect of a role in the resulting project.
- Partner with another agency with the staff and expertise to help you develop and write the application. The key to making this strategy work is negotiating mutually satisfactory roles that also make sense to the funder.

Regardless of which strategy you employ, your partner or partnering agency must be qualified as defined by the funder and the business relationship must be acceptable to the funder. Minimize the likelihood for future misunderstanding by reducing the relationship, roles, and responsibilities to writing at the outset.

28

Get Someone Else to Do
the Parts You Loathe

If you loathe some of the tasks involved in grantseeking, or lack needed skills and have no desire to acquire them, or are simply short on time, why not break down the process into its component parts and get someone else to help you fill in the gaps?

Project components—one or more of which you might outsource to a consultant—include the following major tasks:

- Needs assessment, including key statistics, local/ regional situation, conduct of focus groups, documentation of national/global trends
- Project design, including goal and objective setting, work plans, logic model/evaluation design, relationship to best practices
- Writing the case statement or narrative; organizing the overall proposal and editing it for consistency and responsiveness to funders' requirements
- Funding research
- Budgeting—revenues, including matching funds, and expense projections

29

On the Naming of Grant Projects

When you name your baby—er, grant project—don't get carried away. Apply the five tests of the D-A-M-U-S mnemonic:

1. Descriptive. Of the project, or why bother naming it?
2. Acronyms. Cool, if you can make it work.
3. Memorable. There should be a story behind the name.
4. Unique. Hard to achieve, but worth the effort.
5. Short. One to three words is best, if it gets the job done.

To come up with a project name, identify key words that describe your project, juxtapose and combine these key words (in short, play with the words), and brainstorm potential project names. Test your results on search engines. Consider securing a service mark and reserving a website address.

You can always try out a project name for a few days before making a final decision. Once chosen, the project name needs to be referred to consistently in speech and in written materials. And make sure your name or acronym has no negative associations for funders or the target population.

While we're on the subject of project names, it might be a good time to say a few words about logos, symbols that brand your project. While a logo can wordlessly and power-fully communicate your project, overused designs (such as "hands shaking hands") convey corniness. No- or low-cost, high-quality logo development help can be as close as your local art and design school if you time your request in sync with the academic year.

30

Plan and Prosper

When people who want grant funding tell me "we already have a plan," they often have no more than a vague, unwrit-ten notion of what they want to do. I am tempted to quote the late Dennis Hopper's advice in TV advertisements: "You need a plan."

A plan is a written document that explains how some-thing should happen—in this case, your project. Planning, which is the process that results in a plan, is essential to your grantseeking success because your plan is the basis for your funding proposal. Funders reading your proposal will assess the quality of your plan: in essence, the clarity, com-pleteness, and constructiveness of your thinking.

Planning involves visualization, imagination, and the ability to see your project in the round—that is, from vari-ous perspectives (how it impacts agency staff, the target population, the funder, your board of directors, and so forth).

Planning requires you to make and test assumptions about causation—that is, what makes things happen, to anticipate the future, and to see the big picture while also grasping the details.

Effective planning also entails awareness of the likely relationship between effort and results. You should understand the impact of Pareto Optimality (commonly called the 80/20 Principle) on your project. A valuable and entertaining explanation of Pareto Optimality is provided by Richard Koch in *The 80/20 Principle: The Secret of Achieving More With Less.*

31

Activate a Project Design Team

The collective wisdom of a multidisciplinary project design team can provide you with the diverse perspectives and expertise you need to plan a fundable project.

Ideally, your team will include the following resources:

- Subject matter experts (such as clinicians, social workers, outreach workers, and representatives of the target population)
- Management (reporting relationships, scheduling and timing issues)

- Accounting/financial management (budget, matching funds, and cost-finding issues)
- Human resources (staffing and staff recruiting issues)
- Facilities management (logistics issues)

Small agencies can work around the fact that few of the above disciplines are on staff by reaching out to board members and others to complement in-house expertise.

In a larger agency, where interdisciplinary project planning is a formalized process, you may need to counter the tendency to repeatedly involve the same people in planning. For example, you might get fresh, realistic perspectives on data collection for project evaluation from administrative and clerical staff.

Agency culture determines how you organize and activate your project design team and how you structure your project design process. It should be clear, either from senior management or your own conduct, that you are the team leader. Regardless of the size and resources of your agency, it might help you to think of yourself as leading a virtual project design team that benefits from many kinds of expertise from many experts.

Project design involves answering key questions about the problem or need, then reducing these answers to writing. Your written plan can then be adapted to the specific format and content needs of prospective funders. Several team members may contribute to the written plan, in which case one person has the responsibility of melding the contributions into a document that speaks with one voice.

Group meetings of your team focused on answering key questions can be crucial to developing a sound project design. Don't fall into the time trap of continually postponing team meetings because "Ziggy can't make it this week" (next week Zaggy can't make it). Yes, it will place more of a burden on you as team leader to keep Ziggy and Zaggy informed of the project design process and elicit their input outside team meetings.

32

Project Design: Describe the Problem

Time spent fully understanding the problem or need your project will address is time well spent. This step in the design process is the foundation for all that follows, because your project goals and objectives, intervention strategies or project activities, staffing, budgets, and so forth build on your assumptions and conclusions as to the nature of the problem or need.

Consider the possibility that you don't know all you should about the problem. Jot down what you think you know and ask yourself, "What do I need to know that I don't know yet?" This question leads to others, such as "How and where can I find out what I need to know?" The road to funding is paved with the answers to what are often referred to as "stupid questions," such as:

- Whose needs are we really talking about? Our clients? Our agency?

- What agency data do we have that describes this need or problem?
- What independent data confirms this need or problem?
- What resources that we already have can we redeploy to address this issue—and what are the consequences for our other services?
- Who else in our community faces this issue, and what do they think, or what are they doing, or what have they done about it?
- Who else outside our community faces this issue, and what have they done about it?
- What does the target population think about this issue? Our board of directors? Our staff?
- Why is it important to address this problem? Who should care about it and why?
- What is going on in the environment (i.e., the economy, technological change, social and cultural change) that impacts this problem?
- How have we defined this problem as compared to other agencies that also deal with it?
- How will our mission be fulfilled and our service objectives advanced by this project?

To answer these questions, you may need to make phone calls or site visits, interview agency staff or others, or consult books or Internet search engines.

When you have thoroughly understood the problem or need and described it in writing, you are ready to devise one or more strategies to address it.

33

Project Design: Describe the Solution

Having defined the problem, you either think you know how to solve it or you don't. If you think you have a solution, express it in specific terms, including:

- The project goal, which is a general statement of what you want to accomplish (more complex projects may have multiple goals)
- The project objectives, which are measurable, time-sensitive statements of your intentions that, when accomplished, contribute to achieving the project goal or goals
- The project strategies, which describe the activities you will undertake to achieve the project objectives (include evaluation, dissemination, and sustainability activities)

If you think you understand the problem but are having trouble coming up with a solution, consider the following:

- Imagine the improved state of being you want to achieve.
- Research the state of the art or best practices in your sector to find model approaches. It's likely that someone somewhere has already tried to solve your problem with a grant-funded project. Find them and find out what has happened with their project,

and, if you can, get a copy of their project evaluation. You may ultimately decide to take an entirely different approach to solving the problem, in which case it will be useful to be able to explain to the funder why you need to do something different.

- Engage other agencies or individuals, including the target population and people close to the target population, in sessions designed to seek solutions.

- Determine whether or not the funder has already decided how best to solve the problem. If the latter is the case, and the funder has described its approved approach, the funder merely wants to hire the best qualified applicants to implement per the funder's plan. In this instance, be very careful that the funder's approach is sound, productive for your agency and target population, and doable with the funding available.

- Use creative-thinking strategies, such as brainstorming, to come up with multiple potential solutions that you can further examine or test. There are many books about how to generate ideas or solutions to problems; a personal favorite is *A Whack on the Side of the Head: How You Can Be More Creative* by Roger von Oech.

34

Project Design: Consider the Alternatives

Grantseeking consumes lots of time and attention, so be sure you really need a grant for your project. Consider these alternatives or supplements to grant funding:

1. You might determine that you can launch and sustain the project within your current budget, in which case grantseeking will only delay implementation.
2. Sell unused assets and use the proceeds to fund the project.
3. Eliminate another service or program and replace it with the proposed project.
4. Charge fees to support some or all of the costs of a new service or program.
5. If you are already charging fees, increase them to include the cost of the proposed project.
6. Get a bank loan and pay it off with the fees you charge. This works well when you acquire an asset, such as equipment, with which you create revenue.
7. Request a local, state or federal appropriation (see Strategy #23).
8. Use such sources as Gifts in Kind and NAEIR (National Association for the Exchange of Industrial Resources) to acquire new equipment, supplies, software, and other items.
9. Explore state and federal surplus equipment programs.
10. Recruit volunteer labor and expertise.

11. Improve the efficiency with which you provide the service.

12. Get a third party to pay for a portion of the costs, because the project saves them money in addressing the same problem or need.

13. Identify and secure a major contributor or sponsor (individual or business).

14. Launch a fundraising campaign, beginning with your own board and stakeholders, or hold a one-time or continuing fundraising event.

15. Explore co-marketing arrangements with businesses to create income.

16. Create a for-profit business enterprise and use its income to support your project.

17. Join another agency's proposal as a subgrantee or subcontractor.

18. Combine two or more of these alternatives to assemble sufficient resources.

Think about the nature of your project and what source or sources of funding will best support it. Some projects need only one source of funding, while others may necessitate funding from a variety of sources over time. Even if you ultimately decide to seek a grant or grants, these and other alternatives may contribute to the total resources you have available to sustain the project after grant funding ends.

35

Project Design: Replicate
a Successful Project

The problem or need you have identified has very likely been addressed by others. Why reinvent the wheel if you can replicate a successful project?

Be aware that some funders or grant programs may be focused on funding model approaches that are freshly minted and supposedly "new under the sun." Many others, however, will be impressed by your awareness of what is going on in the world that begins beyond the doors to your agency. They will be interested to see how you have adapted a tried-and-true approach to the particular characteristics of your own agency and service milieu.

How do you find replicable projects? By asking around, usually either through phone calls to other agencies or Internet research. For example, funders may publish descriptions of current or previously funded projects that are similar to your proposed project. Also, summaries of research into the effectiveness of project designs and intervention strategies may be available.*

---

*See, for example, *What We Know Works: An Overview of Research about What Works (and what doesn't) in Social Service Programs,* by the Pew Partnership for Civic Change, 2001.

36

Project Design: To See With New Eyes, Make a "Sight" Visit

Someone, somewhere, is probably operating a project similar to the one you've been dreaming about. That someone probably won't mind your phone call, or even your visit to gather information for your project plan. I have learned more visiting other agencies and programs than I could imagine sitting at my desk. Show your appreciation by bringing a gift for the break room that all can share. Here's a site visit protocol you can adapt to your own needs:

Site Visit Protocol

Agency Name:_____

Agency Address/Phone #s:_____

Host/s and Title/s:_____

Site Visit Date/Time:_____

Site Visitor/s:_____

Planning:

1. Who saw need for this project -- and why was this project needed?

2. How did you develop the project?

3. Why did you take this approach?

4. What other approaches did you consider and why were they rejected?

5. What is the project service area?

6. What is the target population?

7. Did anything special about the target population, service area, or your agency affect project design?

(Continued)

8. How was the community and/or target population involved in project planning?

9. How did you assess needs (methods and documentation)?

10. How were other agencies involved in project planning?

11. Was your project based on other models? If so, where?

Implementation/Operations:

1. What services or programs are offered?

2. Describe the fees, eligibility for services, and admission criteria.

3. How (and how conveniently) does the target population access the services?

4. What other access issues (cost, scheduling, transportation, etc.) have you encountered?

5. To what extent are you attracting populations other than the intended target population?

6. How are services or programs scheduled (hours/days, efficiencies/ productivity)?

7. What major expected problems were encountered during implementation?

8. How were these expected problems dealt with?

9. What major unexpected implementation problems were encountered?

10. What have you done to address these unexpected problems?

11. What information systems integration issues have you experienced?

12. How well are project goals, objectives, and timelines being met?

13. What would you do differently if you had it to do over again?

Staffing:

1. How would you assess the adequacy of staffing versus workload?

2. What qualifications do you look for in selecting staff?

3. What kinds of job descriptions do you use for staff, and what salary ranges are paid?

4. How do you attract staff?

5. Do you experience any extraordinary staff turnover issues; if so, how do you deal with them?

6. How is staff coordination and communication accomplished (meetings, memos, etc.)?

7. Are board members or volunteers involved in staffing?

(Continued)

Management/Monitoring Controls:

1. How do you define a unit of service (encounter, visit, hours of service, etc.)?

2. What kinds of utilization/data reports do you regularly generate or receive?

3. What is the cost per unit of service or cost per client (or other performance indicators)?

4. What kinds of tracking/monitoring systems do you use to manage the project?

5. Do you use written policies and procedures to manage the project?

6. Does your agency generate activity, revenue and expense reports for this project?

7. What kinds of satisfaction surveys (clients, other agencies, etc.) do you utilize?

Coalition Partners (if relevant):

1. Who are your project partners? What are their roles and commitments?

2. How do you keep your project partners informed?

3. How, and how often, do you conduct coalition meetings? How active is attendance and participation?

4. Have you encountered any unusual interagency coordination issues or governance concerns?

Promotion:

1. What promotional and public relations strategies do you use to attract clients, educate the public, generate community support, or keep your funder or funders informed?

2. Can you share any examples of brochures, flyers, posters, public service announcements (PSAs), or news articles, used in the project?

Facilities/Equipment/Technology Vendors:

1. How adequate and accessible are facilities and locations for the target population?

2. Is any special equipment needed to carry out the project?

3. Can you provide any cost or vendor contact information with respect to equipment?

(Continued)

Funding Sources/Sustainability/Dissemination/Evaluation:

1. Funding: Revenue/reimbursement: $_____ and ____percent
2. Funding: Foundation grants: 　　$_____ and ____percent
3. Funding: State/local govt. grants: 　$_____ and ____percent
4. Funding: Federal govt. grants: 　　$_____ and ____percent
5. How have you, or will you, sustain the project without grant funding?
6. How have you disseminated project activity or results?
7. How do you evaluate the project? How often is evaluation performed? By whom? Do you budget for independent evaluation? How are evaluation results documented and used to improve service/program performance?

Documentation:

Business cards

Copy of brochure

Copy of needs assessments

Copy of mission statement, protocols, policies/procedures, job descriptions

Copy of grant application(s)

Copy of evaluation

Copy of utilization and/or annual reports

37

Project Design: Consider Collaboration

Working with other agencies, units of government, businesses, or associations to address a problem or need collectively can be an effective means to win grant money and achieve enduring change. Since many problems fall between the cracks that separate services and programs at multiple agencies, collaboration can lead to solutions based on systemic change. Collaboration may be indicated when a problem:

- Is too big for your agency to handle alone
- Is shared by multiple organizations
- Is getting worse

Potential benefits of collaboration for your agency and other agencies include:

- Successfully addressing seemingly intractable problems
- Access to multiple grants and larger grants
- Economies of scale in addressing big problems

From the funder's standpoint, collaboration can offer:

- More accountability
- Enhanced community involvement
- Higher likelihood of positive results

Major obstacles to collaboration include:

- Lack of trust among potential partners due to past dealings
- Fears of loss of control or loss of "organizational sovereignty"
- The sheer amount of work involved, especially coordination and meeting time

Outside facilitation can be valuable in helping collaborators:

- Define the nature of the problem/need
- Explore alternative strategies to address it
- Develop and negotiate respective roles and resources committed to the project
- Achieve consensus on next steps
- Reduce the meeting of the minds to a memorandum of understanding or memorandum of agreement

Regardless of what you call it—collaborative, cooperative, consortium, partnership, or strategic partnership—in the right circumstances, collective action can help you win grants, build working relationships, and solve problems. Remember Benjamin Franklin's adjuration: "We must all hang together, or assuredly we shall all hang separately."

38

Project Design: Plan for Impediments

Project plans are typically overwhelmingly optimistic. For realism's sake, think like a pessimist. Ask, "What bad things can happen to this project, and what might we need to do to get the project back on track?"

One way to plan for impediments is to "question your answers" at the end of the project design process, and ask yourself and your design team how realistic your expectations are. Ask:

- How much work can be accomplished during a set length of time with certain resources?
- How is the target population likely to respond to changes in the way services are provided?
- How easy will it be to assemble, train, and deploy project staff in the time you have allotted?
- How will you deal with the loss of the project director or other key staff?
- How will you obtain data for project monitoring and evaluation?
- How will you adjust to shortfalls if funding from other sources does not materialize as expected?

As a result of reexamining your project assumptions, you may realize that you need to involve additional people to complete your project plan.

Funders know from experience that projects often go awry. Funders also know that a good project plan anticipates likely obstacles and puts forth strategies to surmount them.

39

Project Design: Work Plan

The work plan shows how you will achieve your project objectives through grant-funded activities (also called tasks, steps, or actions).

Depending on the complexity of the project, the work plan can be as simple as a brief description or list of activities or as complicated as a table such as the one shown below.

Work Plan					
Goal (or problem statement):					
Objectives	Key Action Steps	Expected Outcome	Data, Evaluation and Measurement	Person/ Area Resp.	Timeline

Regardless of whether you explain your work plan in narrative or tabular format, you'll want to show thoughtful distribution of responsibilities among numerous agency staff or partnering agencies (in planning a project, it may help you to keep a list of available staff at hand to use like a "cast of characters" in assigning tasks). The timelines for the completion of project tasks should be realistic, showing sensitivity to potential obstacles, including staffing constraints and holidays. Overall, the work plan should quantify inputs and outputs as much as possible and convince the funder that planned activities, if accomplished, are likely to achieve the project's intended objectives. It may also be advisable to relate goals, objectives, and activities to specific budget line items in order to show grant reviewers how the funder's money helps you achieve the project's aims.

40

Project Design: Budgeting

Your budget should be based on your work plan—what you intend to do—as well as your agency's historical operating costs. Recent agency experience implementing other projects can also be invaluable. Your agency's chart of accounts can serve as a checklist of expenses that helps you identify all of the costs your project is likely to involve.

Participation in the project budgeting process by agency accounting and financial management staff—or other expert resources, such as board members—is critical in developing a budget you can live with if the grant is awarded.

Give special attention to how your proposed project fits in financially with your overall agency activities and budget. Be sure to budget for indirect costs, commonly called overhead or management and general expense, if allowed, and an annual inflation factor for multiyear project expenses.

41

Project Design: Matchmaking

Most funders want you to have some skin in the game. Matching, or cost-sharing, shows them how serious you are about your project, proves you are not totally dependent on the grant, and indicates the potential for sustainability when grant funding ends.

There are two kinds of match: cash and in-kind.

- Cash is real money, the kind you can spend. Cash for match comes from your agency's savings or general revenues or another source that is not restricted to uses unrelated to your grant project.
- In-kind match encompasses a wide array of non-cash resources that you need to accomplish the project, such as personnel and fringe benefits, office space and utilities, and donated products and services.

Successful matching requires creative thinking. The nature and extent of your matching provides clues to the funder about your resourcefulness and the thoroughness of your project planning. You need to take the time to identify all of the resources you need to accomplish your project and distinguish between resources you will:

- Provide with grant funds
- Provide with agency funds (cash match)

- Provide with agency resources (in-kind)
- Provide with other resources (cash or in-kind, perhaps from local supporters)

If you are not an accounting whiz, you will need help in establishing and maintaining documentation—a "paper trail"—that proves your agency fulfilled the matching requirements you promised the funder. If your project involves partnering agencies or businesses that commit matching funds or other resources, you'll need to have the nature, extent, and duration of these commitments in writing.

Two no-no's: you can't promise the same resources twice, and, with few exceptions, you can't use previously awarded public funds to match requested public funds from the same source.

42

Project Design: Sustainability

Funders want to know what happens when their funding ends. Even if they didn't care, shouldn't you? If it's a capital project, how will you finance the ongoing costs of operating the new facility or equipment? If it's a new program or service, how will you keep up the good work? What's your agency's track record in sustaining previous grant-funded initiatives? If you lead a coalition, how will your partners share the responsibility for continuing the project?

Sustainability plans that focus on "winning another grant" to prop up the project are losers. Here are some examples of winning strategies:

- Written letters from your CEO and partnering agencies committing future resources for the project, such as cash, staff time, facilities, and other resources
- A grant-funded outreach initiative could show how newly enrolled clients will be covered by publicly funded programs, thereby creating a sustainable revenue stream that supports expanded services.
- An innovative case management program could demonstrate how its cost-effectiveness will, at best, lead to increased service reimbursement or, at least, lead to lower costs per unit of service.
- An interagency network could show how increased utilization and multiple uses of grant-funded technology lead to reduced unit costs.
- A coalition could show how modest user fees contribute to increasingly diversified revenues over time.

One way to develop your sustainability plan is to uncritically brainstorm a lengthy list of sustainability strategies, then edit the list for realism. Be sure to show how each strategy contributes to the project's overall sustainability and when and by whom each strategy will be implemented.

43

Project Design: Evaluation

The funder wants to know—and you ought to want to know—"Does the project work?" Evaluation is the process that answers that question, along with many other related questions, such as, "How can the project be made to work better?"

The evaluation approach you choose depends on the nature of your project and the funder's requirements. While there are numerous evaluation typologies, evaluation can be described as being primarily "process," "formative" or "summative" in nature:

- Process evaluation focuses on implementation metrics (did you do what you said you'd do when you said you'd do it?) and outputs (did you provide the types and volumes of services you projected?).
- Formative evaluation is used to inform and improve the conduct of the project as it proceeds.
- Summative evaluation involves assessment of the project's ultimate impacts or outcomes.

Evaluation can be conducted internally, by a volunteer advisory body, or by a professional evaluator with whom your agency has contracted. Alternatively, the funder may require participation in a national evaluation. Generally, process evaluation can be conducted internally or by a volunteer advisory body, while formative and summative evaluation necessitates independent professional help.

Consider the following in designing, or contracting for, the evaluation of your project:

- How well do your project objectives lend themselves to measurement? Do they need to be more specific?
- What kinds of data can you collect and aggregate that demonstrate the extent to which the project works? Who will collect this data, and how will they collect it? With respect to data collection and reporting, are there any privacy or workload issues that need to be addressed?
- Are there ways you can incorporate direct feedback from the target population as a means to assess project performance?
- What factors can you identify that are not part of the project design but that may impact project results?
- What kinds of national standards exist that can be used to evaluate your project?
- How can you organize the evaluation process so you can use the evaluation findings and recommendations to improve future project results?

Common project design pitfalls that negatively impact project evaluation include the following:

- Promising unrealistic results: for example, where the funding period isn't long enough to effect measurable change
- Implementing interventions without adequate baseline data, with the result that you won't be able to figure out what, if anything, your project had to do with the results achieved

If the funder expects you to contract for an independent evaluation, try to find out how much of the overall grant you are expected or allowed to allocate to evaluation. The funder may be specific about this or leave it to your discretion. If possible, find a Ph.D.-level evaluator with experience directly related to your kind of project, who communicates clearly and succinctly, as evidenced by examples of prior written evaluations. You should be able to understand what the evaluator says in person and in writing. The earlier you can involve the evaluator in the project design process, the better. Identifying and securing a commitment from a highly qualified evaluator can improve your likelihood of winning grant support by providing strong evidence to the funder that you have the foundation in place for a successful project.

44

Project Design: Dissemination

Dissemination enables you to sow seeds for social change by broadcasting the results of your project. Funders often ask for a dissemination plan for that very reason. It also promotes accountability on your part and prompts kudos for the funder.

To write a successful dissemination plan, you need to focus on society's need to learn from your experience. You can devise dissemination strategies by imagining concentric circles of interest (local, state, regional, national, and global), by identifying the kinds of people and institutions within each circle who will care about your project and then devising the best methods to reach them.

Here are some examples of dissemination methods:

- Presentations to interested groups, such as the target population, civic and fraternal organizations, and those involved in the project planning process
- Presentations and poster sessions at professional conferences
- Newsletters—not only your own agency organ, but also those distributed by and to your peers
- Television and radio interviews and stories showing your project in action
- Print news articles, including business newspapers
- Articles in peer-reviewed (refereed) journals
- White papers, case studies, and one-pagers for distribution to elected officials and other key decision makers
- Web postings, including postings to the funder's website

In your dissemination plan, be as specific as possible about whom you will reach and why, and where, when, and how you will reach them. Show you've allocated staff time for dissemination and, if permitted, that you've budgeted funds for the effort.

Dissemination can result in recognition and respect for you, your agency, your project, and your funder (first, be sure to check to see if and how the funder wants recognition). Dissemination can also help you sustain your project and build upon it by connecting to the wider community of people and agencies that share interests with you. It could even help you attract follow-on funding.

45

Project Design: Finish the Plan Now

If you are having trouble getting started on, or are bogged down in, the project-planning process, here's a trick to try: Imagine your plan is due today and finish it today.* That's right, set an arbitrary deadline and meet it. Find a place where you can work without being disturbed or distracted and focus all your attention on the project. Answer, to the best of your ability and without reference to other people or documents, the key project design questions. Brainstorm multiple strategies. Jot down as many details as you can as quickly as you can.

For simple projects, your day's planning work may be quickly revisable in proposal format. For more complex projects, the result may be a checklist of people and documentary sources you need to consult to develop a strong project plan. In either case, at the end of the day you should be able to see the major outlines of your project and how to finish your plan.

---

*I am indebted to Ethan Rasiel and Paul N. Friga's *The McKinsey Mind: Understanding and Implementing the Problem-Solving Tools and Management Techniques of the World's Top Strategic Consulting Firm*, in which they discuss the McKinsey strategy of "solving the problem at the first meeting."

46

Pilot Test Your Project

Consider whether there is any way for you to pilot test your project prior to applying for funding. A pilot test can provide proof to you as well as to potential funders that your concept is feasible and worthy of a grant. A pilot test can help you identify obstacles to successful implementation of your project, and the consequences of failure are less than with full-blown execution.

47

Overview of the Total Grant Funding Market

Now that you know in detail what you want to do, it's time to find the most likely sources to fund your project. There are seven primary funding sources (four private and three public):

1. Private foundations
2. Company-sponsored foundations
3. Corporate giving programs
4. Community foundations
5. Local government
6. State government
7. Federal government

Most of the private foundations, company-sponsored foundations, and corporate giving programs in the United States—and most of the foundation giving—is concentrated in large cities. If you seek private funding, your best information source is the Foundation Center, which dispenses up-to-date data on private funding through its website (*www.foundationcenter.org*), proprietary databases, print publications, classroom and online training sessions, field offices, and hundreds of cooperating collections in libraries across the country. The Foundation Directory Online is the premier database to use in researching private funding, accessible either through subscription or free at one of the several hundred Cooperating Collection libraries in all fifty states, Puerto Rico, and the District of Columbia. The Foundation Center website includes free online training and free access to basic information on foundations, as well as complete copies of their annual tax filings (990-PFs).

Regardless of whether you seek private or public funding, it is usually better to start grantseeking locally because that is where your agency is known and that is where the problem or need you'll address is most acutely felt.

Some agencies and projects can compete for funding from a broad array of public and private sources, while others may only be attractive to a narrow band of funders. Take time to figure out which public or private sources are most likely to fund your agency and project based on past grant awards in your sector as discernible from funder websites and annual reports. I don't think I can stress enough that a key to grantseeking success is qualifying potential funders based on *their* funding interests.

48

Funding Research: Independent
Private Foundations

Independent private foundations are legal entities organized for socially beneficial purposes, including and especially the conduct of philanthropy.*

Foundations are required, in accordance with Internal Revenue Service regulations, to distribute five percent of their assets annually in the form of various kinds of grants.

In dealing with independent private foundations, it might help for you to think of them as being small, medium, or large:

- Small foundations generally have assets from zilch to several million dollars, no staff or only part-time staff, simple application procedures, no or minimal Web presence, and high responsiveness to personal relationships ("who you know").
- Medium-sized foundations are likely to have full-time staff, more formalized application procedures, assets in the millions to tens of millions of dollars, and a website with useful information.

---

*I've divided private foundations into three targets (this strategy, which focuses on independent private foundations, and the next two strategies, which deal with company-sponsored foundations and community foundations) because their funding interests and behavior are often markedly different. Evaluate your funding needs with reference to each of these three kinds of private foundations, so that you can focus your efforts where they are most likely to be successful.

- Large foundations may have dozens of full-time staff, assets in the hundreds of millions to billions of dollars, highly structured application processes, and highly informative websites.

If your agency has limited grantseeking experience, small local foundations may be the best place for you to begin your search for funding. The foundation decision makers are more likely to be familiar with your agency, and you or your agency board members are more likely to know people who serve on the foundation's board of directors.

49

Funding Research: Company-Sponsored Foundations

Company-sponsored foundations are legally independent of the company that established them and are required to file federal 990-PF tax forms. Nevertheless, effective control of the foundation is in corporate hands, and funding priorities and geographic coverage are typically aligned with the company's business interests.

The best way to find out about company-sponsored foundations is through the Foundation Directory's database, as noted in Strategy #47, or through its separate, smaller Corporate Giving Online database, which is solely focused on company-sponsored foundations and corporate-giving programs. There are many other sources of corporate giving information; key ones are listed on the Foundation Center website. You may also be able to learn much more by familiarizing yourself with the company-sponsored foundation's website if there is one.

50

Funding Research: Corporate Giving Programs

Corporate giving programs include contributions of cash and in kind resources, including office or work space, equipment, and donated expertise and services. Since these giving programs are tied directly to the company, generosity is directly dependent upon the company's ongoing profitability.

For companies, corporate giving programs support their business enterprise by enhancing their visibility and public relations in the communities where they do business. Your key to winning corporate donations is showing the company how your agency or project helps them: for example, through the ways it supports the company's employees and their families. This is a situation in which who you know and who knows you can determine whether you get funds. Typically, company public relations departments will be your point of contact.

If your agency is based in a rural area, you may be able to readily identify local companies with corporate giving programs. Otherwise, the most cost-effective way to research corporate giving programs is to buy a subscription to the Foundation Directory online and search the database as instructed, or access the directory for free at one of the Foundation Center's hundreds of Cooperating Collections. Generally, the larger the company, the more likely it is to put its corporate giving program information on the Web.

51

Funding Research: Community Foundations

Community foundations invest funds from multiple contributors (including individuals, families, corporations, and nonprofit organizations) and make grants in defined geographic areas, typically within a metropolitan area, county, region, or in some cases on a statewide basis. According to the Foundation Center, there were more than 700 community foundations in the United States in 2008.

The Council on Foundations, at *www.cof.org*, offers an online map you can use to see if there is a community foundation that makes grants in your location.

Although community foundations award a miniscule proportion of private foundation grants, their giving is growing rapidly and may represent an important source of funding in your location and for your project.

Generally, the larger the community foundation, the more information you can find out about its grant-making philosophy and history. Also, the larger it is, the more likely it is to have formalized application processes, such as request for proposal, or innovative approaches to funding such as giving circles, wherein contributors pool their money to make strategic awards for community-enhancing projects.

52

Funding Research: Local Funding

Grant funding from your county or municipality may be available depending on your location, your agency's activities, the local government budget, and other factors. As with funding from state government, don't overlook what are termed contracting opportunities.

Local government may administer federal pass-through funding in the form of block grants relevant to your agency and project. Check with your city or county on availability, eligibility, timelines, and requirements.

To find out about local funding:

- Use the Catalog of Federal Domestic Assistance to identify pass-through funding programs.
- Check your city or county website.
- Talk with local government officials.

Generally, the larger the jurisdiction's population, the more funding available and the more sophisticated the grant process. For example, some rural counties may have virtually no funding on offer, but the City of New York provides funding to local cultural agencies to the tune of $150 million annually.

Be prepared to get in line—and it may be a long line—because you may be entering an annual competition and seeking to disturb long-standing local funding patterns. You'll also need to be ready to plead your case with elected officials and the general public; your board of directors and volunteers may help you with this process.

53

Funding Research: State Funding

State governments offer grants funded from in-state tax revenues and distribute grants from federal funding, also called pass-through grants. Other sources of state funding include contracts to provide services and directed appropriations.

In general, states have not fully automated grantseeking and grants management processes. The maintenance and updating of online databases and references listing state government grant opportunities may fall victim to budget deficit reduction initiatives or changing priorities. For example, the state of Georgia's Catalog of State Financial Assistance Programs was last published nearly a decade ago.

Information about state grants may include the following sources:

- State Register
- State business daily or electronic business daily
- State agency and department websites
- Email alerts from a grantmaking state agency
- Online research into state agencies followed by phone calls or visits

Key characteristics of state grant funding can be summarized as follows:

- Detailed application guidelines, often resulting in deliverables-based contracts
- Highly detailed reporting requirements
- Worthy of attention due to the number of federal pass-through grants distributed by states

54

Funding Research: Federal Funding

The federal government offers billions of dollars in grants each year for a broad array of one-time and multi-year projects. Some grant programs have been available for decades.

In response to federal law, and as part of its effort to "streamline and simplify" grant funding, the federal government offers an increasingly automated grant funding process through its Web portal. At *www.grants.gov* you can:

- Research funding opportunities
- Sign up to get email alerts on new grant opportunities
- Register your agency
- Apply for funding
- Track your applications after submittal

Key characteristics of the federal grant-funding apparatus can be summarized as follows:

- Highly detailed application guidelines that reference similarly detailed regulations and enabling legislation
- Highly detailed grant performance and reporting requirements
- High transparency as compared to foundations and state and local funders

There is a seemingly endless array of information sources about federal grant-making. Here are three important ones:

- Catalog of Federal Domestic Assistance, at *www.cfda.gov*, a searchable database that provides essential information on 2,112 federal assistance programs at latest count

- Federal Register, at *www.federalregister.gov*, the official publication for proposed and final rules, notices, and other publications of federal agencies
- Electronic access to a broad array of federal information is also available through FDSys, at *www.gpo.gov/fdsys*.

Federal grantseeking requires patience and attention to minutiae. Grant guidelines tend to be excruciatingly thorough. Entire sections of the guidelines may not even apply to your type of agency or project; over time, you will develop the ability to skim quickly and see through the gray to the green.

Historical information about long-standing grant programs is usually available, and it can be valuable in deciding whether to devote the substantial time needed to develop federal grant applications. You can often find abstracts of funded projects, thereby gleaning information about funding patterns and trends. Federal employees are accessible by phone and email, but be prepared for any contact by reading the guidelines and federal department website carefully.

Due to the legislative basis for federal grant programs and the national competition for limited funds, winning your first award may seem daunting—but it happens every day. Be aware that many awards hinge on qualifying for preference points or showing that your request addresses funding priorities. Sometimes, projects with excellent reviewer ratings aren't funded when federal departments lift projects from historically less-funded or poorer states above the "pay line" to achieve geographic equity.

Some people find federal grantseeking frustrating, intimidating, and downright Byzantine. Others relish the competition, and accept and even appreciate the relative impersonality and lack of cronyism at the federal level as compared to some other funding sources.

55

Funding Research: If You Want the Scoop, Get in the Loop

If you hear about grant funding opportunities shortly before the due date, you aren't giving yourself a fair chance to win. Don't depend on expensive, hard-copy grant-funding newsletters, which may reach you too late. Instead, troll the websites of funders of interest to you for news and get on any listservs offered.

Familiarize yourself with funders' Web postings. More and more foundations have well-maintained sites. For federal funding, get to know your way around *www.grants.gov*. State governments' funding information is also increasingly found online.

If public funding is part of your plans, be aware of municipal, county, state, and federal budget cycles. Many public grant programs are renewed year to year without substantive changes, so you can and should plan your project well ahead of the formal funding announcement. Some funders, especially public agencies, hold regional meetings to promote grant opportunities, while others present at professional conferences.

56

Funding Research: Dialing for Dollars

Sometimes phoning funders will provide you with crucial information about grant opportunities, and sometimes it won't. For various reasons, some funders won't talk to you (they're understaffed or too busy, or they work for a state agency that prohibits them from talking to you about open grant opportunities, etc.). If you decide to call:

- Read the funder's website thoroughly before you call. Funder staff won't want to be schmoozed for information that would-be grantees were too lazy to learn there.
- When you call, briefly summarize
  - ○ Who you are
  - ○ The name and location of your agency
  - ○ The reason for your call
- If you are seeking clarification on a current grant opportunity, have the specific page and paragraph to which your question relates ready for reference. However, some funders will only respond to emailed or faxed questions that are then published with responses for all applicants to see.
- The funder may tell you about upcoming but as yet unannounced grant opportunities, in which case you'll want to probe for estimates on when the grant will be announced, the eligibility requirements, the total grant program budget, and the likely number of grant

awards. Don't push your luck by peppering funder staff with a jillion questions. Just get all the information you can.

- If you want to know if the funder will consider your project, briefly describe what you want to do and its significance in terms of the funder's mission, but avoid lengthy, detailed descriptions unless prompted by the funder's questions.

57

Design the Project to Fit the Funding Criteria

This strategy—which amounts to reverse engineering—works best with public funding because the grant guidelines are often highly prescriptive in accordance with enabling legislation and agency administrative regulations.

If the funding agency spells out in detail what they want, think backwards from their requirements to a project design that preserves the spirit of *your* project within the letter of *their* guidelines.

It alternately irritates and heartens me to read 150 pages of grant guidelines. Yes, the guidelines are often longer than the response allowed, and thank goodness for that. I am irritated because I know I need to go over the guidelines carefully, and care takes time. I am heartened because I know that the funder is telling me what to say and how to say it to win the grant.

58

Attend a Free Grant Opportunities Workshop

When funders offer free workshops to describe their grant-making plans, it's a great chance for you to acquire the following information:

1. Their grant-making strategy: what they are trying to accomplish with grants and what kinds of projects they will fund
2. Grant program contacts
3. Specifics on upcoming grant opportunities
4. Their annual grant competition and grant-making timetables and funding budgets (how many dollars they expect to award for each program, the number of awards and average size of awards)
5. Grant-writing tips based on perhaps hundreds of prior applications; how they evaluate and score applications
6. Grant accounting, reporting, and other compliance issues, including the most frequent problems the funder encounters with grantees
7. Who else is competing with you for funding. You can learn a lot from the questions others ask and the answers they get from grant program staff.

You can find out about grant workshops directly from funders or via your senator's or congressman's office. (These offices sometimes co-sponsor workshops with federal agencies.) In some cases, workshops focus on a single grant program or agency, and in other cases, multiple agencies and programs may be presented.

One of the best things about these workshops is that they give you an informal opportunity to meet funders' grant program staff and get feedback on your pet project, including ways to make it more competitive.

SECTION TWO
Persuade

59

Five Key Questions to Ask About Every Grant Opportunity

By now you've identified the main public and private sources of grants for your agency. You're reviewing new grant opportunities regularly and deciding—perhaps in consultation with others at your agency—whether to move ahead with an application. You should answer a strong "yes" to each of the following key questions:

1. *Are you eligible?* First and foremost, your agency should clearly meet the funder's legal status requirements. Second, if the funding program has been offered before, there may be Web-accessible lists of grantees that show what kinds of agencies have been funded in the past. If your agency is not eligible for direct funding, you may be able to partner with an appropriate applicant agency and subcontract a significant portion of the project.

2. *Is the grant aligned with your agency mission and goals?* Once you're sure your agency is eligible for funding, consider how closely the grant matches your agency's purpose and plans. I feel positive when I hear agency management say, "We're going to pursue this project regardless of whether we win the grant because it makes good business sense. The grant will just help us do it sooner."

3. *What are your chances?* You'll want to be well positioned to win based on your agency's qualifications, the problem or need you've defined, and the project you've designed. If possible, get a sense of the number of likely applicants versus the number of available grants. Grants with a Web-accessible record showing abstracts of previously funded projects enable you to gauge whether your proposed project is likely to appeal to the funder (also, some programs report the percentage of prior applicants who won each round of funding).

4. *Is it worth the trouble?* The funding agency should clearly explain what they want you to include in your application, and they should offer enough funding to do the job right. How much money has been allocated for the entire grant program? How much for each project? Can your agency comply with grant reporting, project evaluation, cash or in-kind matching, and other requirements—especially if they involve multiyear commitments—and are these requirements reasonable given the funding level?

5. *What happens when the grant ends?* Funders want to know your game plan for sustaining the project when grant funding ends. If the grant pays for new equipment, can your agency support the ongoing equipment maintenance expenses? If the grant is for programs or personnel, how will your agency continue these activities on a long-term basis? You'll need a convincing sustainability plan, so convince yourself first.

60

Read the Instructions

Read the grant application guidelines at least three times before you begin developing your application:

- First, read quickly to get an overall sense of what the funder is looking for and how well it aligns with your agency's needs. At this point, you can use the five criteria described in Strategy #59 to make a go or no-go decision.
- Once you've decided to move ahead, read the guidelines slowly and carefully to develop a checklist so you can be sure you address all the requirements, issues, and questions. If the funder references national studies or its own reports or studies as the basis for the grant program, be sure you find and read this reference material.
- Finally, read the guidelines once again to make sure you didn't miss anything. It is easy to miss crucial information embedded within long-winded, poorly organized, repetitive grant guidelines. Also, be sure to check the funder's website frequently to see if the funder issues modifications that change, correct, or clarify the grant guidelines.

61

Get Clarification

After you read the grant guidelines, you are bound to have questions. Get the answers to your questions early in the grant development process by the following methods:

- Thoroughly read the funder's website. Funders increasingly post FAQs (Frequently Asked Questions) and responses to these questions. You'll want to recheck the funder's website periodically to see if they update their FAQs prior to the application deadline.
- Phone or email the funder after writing down your questions as concisely as you can.
- Attend preproposal meetings in the flesh or over the phone and Web. If you attend these sessions, you are likely to pick up information that never makes it into the written guidelines (voice intonations, informal comments, etc.). Your competitors' questions and the fact of their attendance will also give you information. Just don't be intimidated by the occasional know-it-all.

62

Keep on Track with a Tracking Tool

A simple table like the one shown below can help you keep up with the people and agencies involved in your project. You can add columns to track the status of such items as letters of commitment and support, signature approval on a memorandum of understanding, and data or verbiage requested for inclusion in a grant proposal.

Tracking Tool							
Agency Name and Address	CEO/ Other Name and Title	Phone Cell Fax Email	Assistant Name and Title	Phone Cell Fax Email	Addl. Agency Contacts and Titles	Phone Cell Fax Email	Status/ Comments

63

The One-Pager

The one-pager is an educational tool that enables you to explain your project briefly and to advocate for it with people whose endorsement or assent you need to move ahead, including:

- Board members
- Elected officials
- Partnering agencies and referral sources
- People from whom you want a letter of support
- People from whom you want matching funds or an in-kind contribution

When you write the one-pager (also referred to as a project summary), you are forced to boil your project down to its essentials. It is the written equivalent of the elevator speech and complements it nicely by providing written documentation of your plans. Include the following items in bulleted format:

Project title
Date

- Executive Summary: Brief paragraph or one sentence project summary (for example, "DOFLAGIT, a consortium of public safety agencies, seeks federal

grant funding to complement local taxpayer commitments for a regional, interoperable communications system and asks for your written support for
this request.")
- The problem or need addressed by the project and
  why it is important
- Brief background information, such as target
  population characteristics and service area demo-
  graphics
- Who's applying for funds, including names of partnering agencies and contacts at each agency
- Details about the funding source, amount requested,
  and how funding will be used
- Local supporters and resources already committed
  to the project
- Action requested (for example, letter of support),
  contact information, and deadline

The one-pager will probably be all the information most
busy people need about your project at this point in its
development process—don't tell them more than they want
to know. You can also use it as a checklist when you prepare
your project abstract or executive summary.

64

Master the Letter of Inquiry

The letter of inquiry is increasingly required as a first step in seeking foundation funding.* It enables you to find out if the funder is sufficiently interested in your project to review a more detailed proposal. In short, it saves time for both parties (more for the foundation, since it's easier to read the letter than write it—but then, you're the one who wants money). In fairness to funders, I should add that some letters of inquiry are no doubt painful to read for reasons other than the extremity of need described by the writer. But I digress, something you must never do in your letter, which should be no more than three pages. In essence, the letter of inquiry is to the full proposal as the sizzle is to the steak.

How do you know if a letter of inquiry is indicated? From your funding research or the funder's website, if they have one. The Gates Foundation, for example, lists its criteria for evaluating letters of inquiry. What do you include in your letter? The best explanation I have seen about how to develop an effective letter of inquiry is on the Foundation Center website (*www.foundationcenter.org*) under Frequently Asked Questions. This brief gem of an article also directs you to links with examples of letters.

---

*Public funders, especially state and federal funders, sometimes request a letter of intent with brief information about your plans to apply for an announced funding opportunity. The letter (or increasingly, email) of intent gives the project officer an estimate of the likely volume of incoming responses to the grant opportunity.

65

The Proposal and Its Parts

There is no standard proposal format universally approved by all private funders, although some groups of private funders, such as regional associations of grant makers (RAGs), have agreed on a consistent format. Public funders typically provide highly detailed application formats. The table below is useful in developing a draft proposal that can be adapted to the content and format requirements of virtually any funder.

Proposal Format		
#	Section Heading	Contents Summary
1	Cover letter	If requested; includes a brief summary of your request
2	Abstract/Executive Summary	1-2 pages if requested (see Strategy #66); includes project title
3	Problem/Need Statement	Description of the nature and impact of the problem/need, societal significance, supporting agency data and independent data confirming the nature and extent of the problem, results of surveys and needs assessments, relation to funder's mission (see Strategy #32)
4	Approach and Work Plan	What you will do and the results you expect to achieve (specific outcomes, who benefits, volumes of services), goals and objectives, activities, timelines, responsible persons, resources utilized, measurement of results; relation to best practices/benchmarks, obstacles to success and strategies to deal with them (see Strategy #33), extent to which your project replicates a successful project elsewhere (see Strategy #35)

(Continued)

5	Qualifications Statement	Proof your agency is capable of implementing this project, based on agency history and achievements, staff and board resources, and agency track record as a steward of grant funds (see Strategy #16)
6	Sustainability	How you will continue the service or program once project funding ends (see Strategy #42)
7	Evaluation	Internal or independent assessment of how well your project works, including who will evaluate, when, evaluation methods, and how you will use the findings and recommendations to improve future results (see Strategy #43)
8	Dissemination	How you will inform others of the project results (see Strategy #44)
9	Budget	Project budget with expenses and matching cash and in-kind resources, including a narrative explanation of the rationale for each item (see Strategy #40)
10	Appendices	As requested, these might include evidence of your agency's legal status, annual agency budget, audited financial statement, list of trustees and their affiliations (see Strategy #16)

66

Writing the Abstract

The abstract is a brief distillation, usually in one or two pages, of your project's essence: its purpose and significance, how it will be conducted, why your agency is qualified to conduct it, and so forth. The abstract may be the most important part of your application because it enables the reviewer to get a quick overview of your entire request.

You write the abstract, which may also be referred to by some funders as a project summary or executive summary, after you've written the rest of the application. At the end of the writing process, you can clearly see your project's most important details.

Funders will usually tell you exactly what they want in the abstract, and it can be challenging to select and present the most important details in the allotted space. Effective abstracts highlight the compelling aspects of the project and engage the reviewer's interest in reading the rest of the request.

67

Budgeting: Not a Dollar More, Not a Dollar Less, Than You Need

If you have worked for a while in a nonprofit setting with scant resources, "making do with less," you may be inclined to low-ball your budget request. Conversely, you may be tempted to ask for more than you need for fear the funder will cut the budget in making an award. Neither approach will help you get funded, because either is likely to raise doubts about the realism of your project design. The funder may have established a maximum grant amount or a range of funding levels based on assumptions about the desired scope and scale of projects. Let that, and your agency's operating expense structure, guide your budget projections. Ask for all the money you need to carry out your work plan successfully—not a dollar less, not a dollar more. Unless instructed otherwise, budget in whole dollars and leave off the cents.

Some grant reviewers start by looking at the budget, because for them it's a snapshot of your true intentions. Your budget should clearly link to your project work plan. For example, if you say you are going to disseminate project results, have you calculated the cost of travel to attend a professional conference where you will present these results? If you don't plan to hire all staff at the beginning of the project period, why would you budget them all to start in Month 1? A budget justification, also referred to as a budget narrative, if requested, can improve your funding prospects by showing that you have carefully prepared your proposal. If you will depend on other funding sources, such as agency reserves or fundraising, to supplement the requested grant, indicate the extent to which these other funds are already committed or likely based on prior experience.

68

Show How Your Project Achieves Others' Goals

If you describe your project in the context of local, regional, state, national, and perhaps even global concerns, you are more likely to be funded.

With aspirations that far exceed their budgets, funders are looking for projects that will, in present-day parlance, "make a difference." Funders will respect you for taking the time and pains to read and reference local, regional, state, national, and global studies and strategic plans. Often, these documents are listed on funders' websites or through links to other sites. By including brief, properly cited references to relevant portions of these documents, you can lend credence to your project and better convey its importance. Show how your project achieves broad societal goals as well as the funder's specific objectives.

69

When You Pass the Point of No Return, Don't Turn Back!

There comes a time in the development of some grant applications when you find yourself drowning in details. You have pulled everything you can think of off the Internet, printed and stacked reams of needs-assessment data, and piled up relevant journal articles. Your case statement or project narrative is a welter of run-on sentences and sentence fragments. The hour grows late and the application deadline looms. You, my friend, have reached the point of no return.

If you ditch the effort now, you'll have lost the umpteen hours you've invested. You could wait for the next funding opportunity to come along and put what you've learned to work, but why wait if you've already done most of your homework? You may be closer to the finish line than you think.

Your situation is akin to what happens when you set out to clean up the clutter in the basement, kitchen, attic, or, in our house, the guest bedroom. You've pulled everything off the shelves and out of the boxes, and you have a big mess on your hands that seemingly defies order. What to do?

Here are five coping strategies:

1. If you can identify "the one big issue" about the project that bugs you (usually some aspect of the project you've avoided dealing with), do something about it now. There may be a design flaw that you know dooms the project: Resolve it yourself, or let your project partners know how you plan to resolve it, or ask for their help. Perhaps deep down you fear there is no meeting of the minds among partnering agencies: Clear the air and reduce the understanding to writing. Maybe you're jumping ahead to write the narrative, work plan, and budget when you need to develop some goals and objectives: Back up. If you tackle the biggie problem you've avoided, the job will get easier.

2. Ask for help. You cannot reasonably expect yourself to be simultaneously a writer, subject-matter expert, statistician, public relations whiz, evaluation design expert, and accounting and financial guru. Yet all of these skills and more are often needed to write a grant application. If you figure out what kinds of help you need and tell other people, then

delegate to them properly and give them sufficient time to respond, you will probably get the help you need.

3. Decide something—anything. That's right, make a decision about some aspect of the project. If you've drafted goals and objectives, play them out to their logical conclusion in the work plan and see if the resulting project design makes sense and makes a compelling case for the funder. Remember, you are just thinking on paper until you submit the application—so start making decisions, knowing you can change them in the final draft.

4. Pile up your mess of information and put it behind you (literally, so you can't see it, else what's a credenza for?). Then take the top item off the pile and place it before you. Read or skim it, mark it up, and make notes on it. If it turns out to be irrelevant to the project, toss it. If it's on point, work it into your narrative and then get it out of your sight. If you repeat this step long enough, you'll work through your mess, finding in the process that the pile was less daunting than you originally thought.

5. Take a little piece of the project and go somewhere else to work on it. Try a place less cluttered and stressful than your desk or workstation, such as your back porch or a coffee house—wherever you feel more relaxed. Work solely on the little piece of the project you've brought along.

70

To Be Believed, Be Specific

If you ask for exactly what you need, you are more likely to get it.*

Inspire the funder's confidence with specifics about the underlying problem or need you want to address. If you are writing a human service needs assessment, for example, your data should reflect the specific target population and geographic area you intend to serve. Provide survey and study data comparing your local situation to state and national averages. Show you are up to date with what's happening in your field by citing the most recent reputable independent information sources you can find that support your assertions.

If you can't find specifics, conduct your own survey or study of the problem and cite your own data. If you intend to serve a target population, involve them via surveys or focus groups in defining the problem and suggesting strategies to address it, then write up the results. If you have done your homework, you will have much more information than the funder wants to review, so pick only the most dramatic and telling details. Like a skillful interviewer, imagine the funder's questions and answer them specifically.

---

*And a tip of the hat to Somerset Maugham, who said, "It is a funny thing about life; if you refuse to accept anything but the best, you very often get it."

71

The Most Basic Form of Human Life: The "Sell"

Convincing a funder to give you a grant is a sales job.

You say you don't like salespeople? Haven't you had both bad and good experiences with salespeople, just as you have with people in other professions?

If you focus on your positive sales experiences, perhaps you'd agree that successful salespeople are able to:

- Inspire trust and address the customer's needs and concerns
- Deal with objections until the customer runs out of reasons not to buy
- Accept failure only in specific instances with individual customers, but never generally: Successful salespeople are persistent.

I suspect that when we say a product or service "sells itself," we mean that it is relatively easier to sell than another product or service. In this instance, the selling process is invisible to the customer, who literally demands to buy. I don't think anything "sells itself," and I think that line of reasoning leads some people, particularly those with a broad self-righteous streak, to think that funders "must" respond with grant support. That sort of thinking leads to failure with funders, followed by excuses for failure.

Although some people are "born salespersons," almost anyone can learn to sell. Sales techniques are taught in classroom settings, through books, tapes, and CDs, and, best of all, through experience and experimentation.

72

Write Now, Edit Later

Writing is an incremental process for most practitioners, a bit like elephant-eating (one bite at a time). If you start early, you can finish early, and you may be pleasantly surprised at how quickly you complete a draft application. It's true that, up against a deadline, you might be able to pull an all-nighter to get the job done. But is this how you want to organize your work and your life? Probably not. Remember Pliny's injunction: "Never a day without a line."

One of the best bits of advice I've ever gotten on writing was from Skip Robinson, author of *A Da Vinci to Die For*. Skip told me that editing one's own writing too early in the writing process is not only depressing, it's inefficient. Why lavish time and attention on perfecting paragraphs and pages of your draft application that you later realize need to be entirely excised?

It's better to push ahead and complete a draft of the entire document, no matter how imperfect, then go back and read it in its entirety and begin your edits.

Also, as you write your draft, you may realize you don't have all the facts at your fingertips. In this case, you can use "xx" to mark the spot for future follow up, and keep moving ahead toward your finished draft. You can also keep a pad next to your PC, or better yet, a file within which to jot your notes when stray thoughts occur to you as you complete the draft.

73

Getting Beyond Writer's Block

The very best advice on writing I have ever read was put into words by Epictetus, a Greek stoic philosopher, who advised, "If you wish to be a writer, write."*

There is a lot written about writer's block, and even a fair amount of opinion to the effect that there is no such thing. And yet, there comes a time for many of us when we can't seem to put into words what we want to say.

If you are having trouble putting your thoughts about your project into words, you may benefit from coping strategies to get you beyond the blockage. When it comes to

---

*Discourses, II, c. 110. Interestingly, Epictetus is believed to have written nothing himself; fortunately his pupil Arrian was a writer. I am indebted to a fellow Baltimorean, H.L. Mencken, for bringing this to my attention in *A New Dictionary of Quotations on Historical Principles from Ancient and Modern Sources*, which he selected and edited.

coping strategies, it's a matter of "different strokes for different folks." I can only tell you that it helps me to:

- Write something, anything, and then improve on it
- Spit out a bulleted list of the points I want to make
  (like this one), then string the bulleted list together
  in sentences
- Avoid checking my email, taking phone calls, and
  answering the doorbell
- Focus solely on a very small piece of the project and
  set a time limit on completing this piece
- Take a break or a walk. Sometimes I think about
  anything but my current writing project; other
  times I take paper and pen and focus my thoughts
  on brainstorming a little piece of the project.
- Go somewhere else to write or at least clear my
  visual field of distractions
- Talk about the project while someone takes notes
- Change what I use to record my words and where
  I record them (for example, from computer and
  screen to pen and paper)
- Remind myself that the order in which I express
  my thoughts can be changed later
- Remind myself that the consequences of failure (of
  my first draft) are inconsequential and, in any case,
  correctable

74

Compelling Case Studies

Case studies—brief, written snapshots that showcase human needs, explain why these needs are important, and how these needs will be met by your project—can be a powerful tool that convinces funders through "the power of example." If presented early in a project narrative, case studies can deepen the funder's understanding of, and enthusiasm for, your project by highlighting its impact on people in need. Case studies, like letters of support, represent testimonial proof that your project is worthy of funding.

75

Answer the Funder's Questions

It's a funding request, not a soapbox, so don't spend so much time telling the funder what *you* want them to know that you neglect to tell them what *they* want to know. Having your say may help you emotionally, but it won't help your agency—financially. So answer their questions, not the ones you think they should have asked. Grant reviewers tend to have highly developed bullshit detectors, so tell the "positive truth" about your project and your agency's qualifications, taking credit where it's due and describing what you're doing to improve where needed.

76

Set the Hook

There's a media expression that "If it bleeds, it leads." If you begin your proposal with a brief, compelling summary of the need for, and significance of, your project, you will markedly improve your funding prospects.

Grab the reader with your first sentence and don't let go. Impel the reader forward from sentence to sentence and paragraph to paragraph with a combination of emotional and factual arguments ("heart and mind") that lead to one logical conclusion: This project must be funded!

To help the reader internalize the need for your project, try these methods:

- Appeal to the senses: taste, touch, sight, sound, and especially smell.
- Convey your passion for your project with your word choices, favor shorter words and sentences, and use the active voice whenever possible.
- If permitted by the grant application guidance, insert a text box quoting an independent, respected source that confirms the seriousness of the need.

- When you make a bold assertion, follow it with tabular data, graphs, or a reference to an independent authority that proves your assertion.
- Funders increasingly support efforts to address the most acute needs and mitigate the most alarming disparities, so figure out what makes your situation, your project, your agency, and your community unique or unusually worthy of support; then showcase these characteristics.

77

The Point, and How to Get to It

Funders have a lot of money but no more time than anyone else. They will appreciate it if you get to the point quickly about your project and your funding needs.

When you have a detailed project plan, distill your request into a few concise, compelling sentences.

Your two or three sentence summary should explain:

- The need for your project
- Why your project is important
- Why your agency is uniquely qualified to implement this project
- What you'll do and how you'll do it
- The results you expect

Avoid overlong sentences. Try out your project description—essentially a "sales pitch" or "elevator speech"—on a colleague, and on someone who doesn't know anything about what you do. Does it make sense to them? Can they explain it back to you? Is it conversational, intriguing, and thought- and question-provoking?

If you're having trouble getting to the point, read Milo Frank's classic *How to Get Your Point Across in 30 Seconds or Less*. It's sure to help you, and it's a quick read.

78

"The Perfect is the Enemy of the Good"*

We are often exhorted to "be the best," instructed that "only the best is good enough," and advised to identify and follow "best practices."

Unfortunately, the encouragement of excellence causes self-doubt and hesitation in some people. When it comes to competing for grants, they give up too soon. Unless there is only one grant to be awarded by the funder, you don't have to have the best proposal. Remember that often "the perfect is the enemy of the good." Your best may not be perfect, but it only needs to be good enough to get funded.

---

* So said Voltaire, who also said, "The secret of being a bore is to tell everything."

79

How to Edit Your Proposal

Regardless of whether you've just finished a one-page letter of inquiry, a five-page foundation proposal, or a 200-page federal grant application, you need to edit your writing before unleashing it on the funder.

Here's a three-step approach:

1. First read the entire document yourself, imagining yourself as a reviewer:
   - Does it make a clear, compelling case for funding?
   - Does it respond fully to the grant guidelines?
   - How can it be shortened?
   - Is jargon used sparingly?
   - How can sentence length be varied (short and long)?
   - If the proposal was developed by several writers, does it read with one voice and use consistent terminology?
   - Does it avoid the passive voice? (After all, David Farragut didn't say, "The torpedoes should be damned," nor did Dirty Harry say, "My day will be made by you.")
   - Is there anything in it that might needlessly aggravate the reviewer? For example, such introductory throat-clearing phrases as "arguably," "clearly," "obviously," and "to be sure."

- Does it maximize visual appeal by respecting the funder's formatting requirements? (BELIEVE IT OR NOT, SOME GRANT APPLICANTS SEND REQUESTS PRINTED IN ALL CAPITAL LETTERS AND EXPECT TO BE FUNDED. Don't do it.)

2. Then ask a subject-matter expert to read and comment on the proposal's accuracy and completeness, as well as the soundness of the project design compared to benchmarks, best practices, and current research findings.

3. Finally, ask someone with no specialized knowledge of the subject matter to read and comment on the proposal.

One more suggestion: Sometimes you will find a socko sentence or even paragraph several pages into your draft that deserves to be moved up to page one, where reviewers are more likely to see it (see Strategy #76: Set the Hook).

80

Get an Earful: Read Your Draft Aloud

Since you read with your ears as well as with your eyes, you might also benefit by reading the narrative portions of your proposal aloud or having someone read it aloud to you.

When you hear what you've said, you will see how to say it more concisely and forcefully—in short, more effectively. You may rediscover that shortness of sentences prevents shortness of breath.

81

Superlatives Arouse Suspicion

In presenting your agency's qualifications to the funder, you may be tempted to characterize your agency as "innovative" or "unique"* and your project as a "best practice" or "national model." Use such descriptions sparingly, even if they're true.

It's more likely that what makes your agency special, though perhaps not unique, is its service record, outstanding stewardship of funding, service area characteristics, or the compelling and abiding needs of the target population your agency serves.

If your agency is positively remarkable, provide specifics (examples include utilization levels, productivity, low costs per unit of service delivered, stellar performance evaluations). If your agency is licensed, certified, or accredited by an independent entity, by all means bring it up.

---

*Agencies or projects described as "very unique" are rarer still—rarer, in fact, than unicorns.

If you are convinced that your project is one of a kind, you need to explain why this is true. On the other hand, some funders would be delighted to hear, instead, about how your project is based on a model proven to work elsewhere, but adapted to the special characteristics of your community and target population.

82

Go Light on the Lingo

The use of jargon can save time by enabling people who share a knowledge base to reference commonly understood technical terms about a profession or other activity. It can also flummox or frustrate people who don't know what's being talked about, such as reviewers reading a grant request.

In technical proposals, specialized terminology may be essential to explaining your project design. In this instance, you will know at the outset that your proposal will be peer-reviewed.

If, however, your grant request will be reviewed by generalists (including other people who write grant applications), jargon can cause confusion if not used with restraint. As you edit your funding request, make sure you define unusual terms and acronyms the first time you use them or provide a glossary. You may also need to translate key terms when writing for an audience with varying foreign-language skills.

83

Give Your Proposal Curb Appeal

Some funders will tell you exactly how they want your proposal to look; others won't. In either case, to make your grant
request visually attractive to reviewers, consistency is king:

* Use standard type styles, such as Times New Roman
  and Arial, and fonts no smaller than 12 point, as well
  as black ink and generous margins.
* If tables, graphs, and other figures are allowed, use
  them if they help you prove your points. Be sure
  you label them and reference them in the text. In
  presenting work plans, you can make it easier for
  reviewers to understand complex projects by insert-
  ing a table that shows goals and objectives, activities,
  timelines, responsible parties, resources committed,
  and measures of achievement (see Strategy #39).
* If indicated by the subject matter, you might insert
  quotes from local, regional, and national independent sources that underscore the need for your
  project.

84

Be Merciful to Reviewers

It would be nice if funders said, "We have a couple million to give out in thirty days, so, bearing in mind that brevity is the soul of wit, send us a one-page proposal describing your project, and be sure to tell us how much money you need."

Instead, funders typically want—and need—more details. It's a challenge to respond to grant application requirements concisely and completely, but it's essential to your success.

As you edit your proposal, imagine you are reviewing your own application. You are sitting in a hotel meeting room at one of many round tables with dozens of other grant reviewers. Tall stacks of funding requests lie before you; some of them are very thick. You and your colleagues are about to read all of them and pick the few winners. How much might you and your fellow reviewers appreciate reading a brief, factual, compelling request? Perhaps enough to fund it ahead of other worthy requests that tire your eyes and test your patience.

85

Offer a Good Buy

If you look at your funding request from the funder's stand-point, it's a purchase they want to make wisely. Funders work under the prudent buyer concept: They want to pay no more than a prudent buyer would reasonably expect to spend for a project like yours, including all of its labor and material inputs.

Often, funders have a very good idea of reasonable costs based on historical data for hundreds of similar projects. For example, "The following figures are provided as a guideline in developing the Federal budget request: $150 Federal grant dollars per general community user, $200 Federal grant dollars per migrant/seasonal farmworker user, $200 Federal grant dollars per public housing user." [Source: U.S. Department of Health and Human Services, Health Resources Administration, Bureau of Primary Health Care, New Access Point grant guidelines, October 6, 2006, p. 13.].

Simple measures include cost per unit of service or per unduplicated user. Be sure you adapt your proposal to use the funder's terminology, and use that terminology consistently (visits, encounters, sessions, hours of service, and so forth).

If your costs are substantially lower or higher than typical costs, you need to explain the reasons for the difference. Costs can vary considerably from one part of the country to another, as well as over the course of a multiyear grant, and these variations should also be explained. In general, costs are subject to cross-cutting effects over time: Annual inflation in salaries and other inputs increase costs, while productivity gains dampen cost increases. Multiyear grant funding may be flat from year to year or may increasingly put the onus on the grantee to sustain the project when funding ends. Explaining how changing costs relate to sustainability can give your proposal a competitive edge.

The true "bang for the buck" lies in the social benefits your project brings—its results. Quantifying outcomes may not be easy, but it is nearly always feasible if you work at it. It's likely that researchers and national associations have developed data on the value of your agency's services to society. Also, although human life is priceless, insurance companies and courts of law have imputed financial values to loss of life or lost years of life, loss of wages, and even loss of consortium (loss of the benefits of family relationships). Seek out independent data and use it to quantify the compelling case for your project.

86

Gather Evidence of Support and Commitment

Funders often ask for letters of support or commitment as proof of the extent to which other people, typically people in your community, think your project is needed.

Letters of support confirm the need for your project and your agency's qualifications to carry it out. Detailed support letters that show the supporter deeply understands the need and endorses your agency's approach to the project can be highly effective despite the lack of promised financial or other resources. For example, the parent of a child with special needs can provide anecdotal evidence and unique perspectives based on daily experience.

Letters of commitment promise specific resources, such as a cash or in-kind match, or cooperative actions that assure the funder the project will succeed.

Letters of support or commitment should be on letterhead (with the exception of letters from clients), dated, and signed. Never use a template that is simply photocopied and signed by supporters—this tells the funder nothing other than that you are lazy.

To get a good response:

- Ask long before the grant deadline and be prepared to answer questions about the project the first time you call or email.
- Use your one-pager to provide key details and contact information (Strategy #63).
- Ask if you can help by drafting a letter and emailing it for approval.

Substantive, specific, individual letters of support or commitment can differentiate your grant request from the competition by showing that your agency is known and respected by clients, relevant agency chief executive officers, the business community, civic organizations, and elected officials.

87

Button-Up Checklist

While you are working on your application, it helps to keep at hand a list of reminders keyed to the grant guidelines so you can be sure you take care of every little detail before you finish and submit your application. This is especially the case with government grant applications. Try adapting the list below to fit your project. (You won't need anything this detailed for most foundation proposals.)

		Button-Up Checklist
☐	1.	Final incorporates draft comments by our agency and coalition partners?
☐	2.	Responsive to all grant guidelines, regulations, application questions?
☐	3.	Responsive to all review criteria; visual cues included for reviewers?
☐	4.	Abstract/executive summary concise, compelling, "makes the case"?
☐	5.	Narrative: minimal jargon, acronyms explained, mix of short and long sentences, speaks with one voice?
☐	6.	Visually interesting (graphs, maps, sidebars, indents, headings, bullets, etc., if allowed)?
☐	7.	Charts/tables for goals and objectives, activities/tasks, responsible staff, timelines, measures of achievement?
☐	8.	Correct and complete internal references to tables and figures, attachments, appendices?
☐	9.	Goals and objectives, timelines, budget, evaluation, etc., tie together?
☐	10.	Budget forms and budget justification complete; all calculations foot correctly?

(Continued)

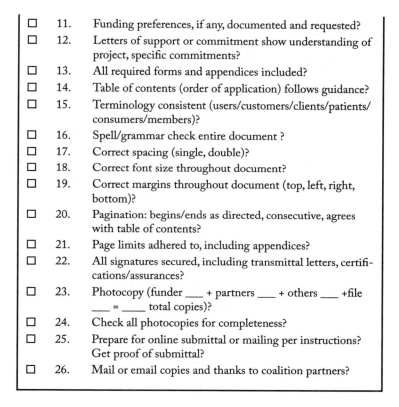

□ 11. Funding preferences, if any, documented and requested?

□ 12. Letters of support or commitment show understanding of project, specific commitments?

□ 13. All required forms and appendices included?

□ 14. Table of contents (order of application) follows guidance?

□ 15. Terminology consistent (users/customers/clients/patients/consumers/members)?

□ 16. Spell/grammar check entire document ?

□ 17. Correct spacing (single, double)?

□ 18. Correct font size throughout document?

□ 19. Correct margins throughout document (top, left, right, bottom)?

□ 20. Pagination: begins/ends as directed, consecutive, agrees with table of contents?

□ 21. Page limits adhered to, including appendices?

□ 22. All signatures secured, including transmittal letters, certifications/assurances?

□ 23. Photocopy (funder ___ + partners ___ + others ___ +file ___ = ____ total copies)?

□ 24. Check all photocopies for completeness?

□ 25. Prepare for online submittal or mailing per instructions? Get proof of submittal?

□ 26. Mail or email copies and thanks to coalition partners?

We are in a transition period between traditional hard-copy grant applications and electronic submittal. As electronic submittal becomes the norm, you'll still benefit from a button-up checklist. Even though online application formats may not allow you to submit the application until all sections are completed, you are still responsible for complying with format and content requirements.

Whether you submit online, via snail mail, or overnight courier, you'll want to get and keep hard-copy proof of delivery. While it's true that the funding agency could still dispute that your overnight package contained a grant application, it's not likely you sent them a rubber chicken.

88

Finish the Darn Thing and Submit It

Management gurus agree: Execution is crucial to success. Such experts as Woody Allen ("Eighty percent of success is showing up") and Wayne Gretzky ("You miss one hundred percent of the shots you don't take") stress the simple advice that you must be in it to win it.

If you are a dithering dreamer or procrastinating perfectionist, do the best you can in the time allotted with the resources available and risk rejection, which is inevitable at least some of the time in this sloppy world.

So finish the darn grant application and send it in.

89

Multiple Submissions

You may need to request support from multiple funders in the following situations:

1. Your initial request, typically to your best funding prospect, is turned down or not fully funded. If the funder's answer is no, or if you receive partial funding, you then adapt your proposal and send it

to your next best prospect, continuing this process until you win full funding. The problem with this serial approach is that you may wait many weeks or months to hear from each funder before going on to the next prospect in the event of failure or partial success. Instead, you may be able to submit requests simultaneously to multiple funders, informing each funder of your other requests. Be aware that, in some cases, particularly public funding, the funder will have rules that prohibit you from "shotgunning" the same request simultaneously to multiple portions of a large grant program.

2. Your project is too large for one funder to handle or lends itself to multiple funders, or your key prospective funder limits its participation to only a portion of your total project costs. In these instances, you may need to secure "anchor" funding from a large, well-respected funder, especially one that cherishes the primary supporting role, and then seek additional funding from other sources for other phases or segments of the project. Alternatively, you might seek modest feasibility study or pilot test funding from a small, local funder and then pursue a larger award to fully implement your project based on the results of your feasibility study or pilot test. In either case, you should be up front with prospective funders about your overall funding strategy and efforts to secure funds.

90

Hosting the Funder's Site Visit

The funder may conduct a site visit before making a decision as to whether to fund your project. The site visit enables the funder to learn more about your agency and project than can be gleaned solely from your written application.

When you agree to the site visit date and learn the duration of the visit, get any additional guidance you can from the funder:

- Who will represent the funder?
- Who from your agency should attend?
- Who else would the funder like to meet, such as agency clients, board members, or partnering agencies?
- What topics would the funder like to discuss in greater detail?
- Will the funder desire or need a facility tour?

Since it may be quite some time since you made your funding request, it could be helpful to gather together your project design team and others who will represent your agency at the site visit and go over the details of your project.

It would be a mistake to orchestrate the site visit to the point that the funder feels manipulated. The funder should see your agency as it is and your people as they are. Remember to introduce your agency representatives. Be prepared to talk about your project in detail, but don't bore the funder with lengthy, canned presentations that leave little time for questions and discussion. Within the context of the limited time during which the site visit will occur, anticipate the funder's needs for refreshment and comfort with the same kind consideration as you would for a guest in your home.

There is no guarantee that what seems to you to be a friendly, businesslike site visit will lead to funding. On the other hand, if you have satisfied the funder's curiosity and concerns about your agency and project, the site visit may be a factor that inclines the funder toward making an award.

91

If at First You Don't Succeed . . . Apply, Apply Again

Sometimes you do everything right—or you *think* you did everything right—but you don't get funded. What can you do?

1. You can try to find out how you can make your application more competitive (this is generally easier with public funders), then revise it as indicated and resubmit it in the next funding cycle if there is one. Conversely, if you're convinced you did a good job, and the funding guidelines haven't changed, you can make minimal changes, such as

updating support letters, and resubmit it in the
next funding cycle.
2. You can submit your application to another funder
   after having adapted it to meet their requirements.
3. You can totally rethink and redesign your project
   and submit it to the same or another funder. This
   is what you do when you reach the conclusion that
   your original project design was flawed.

Forget filing a complaint or similarly making a nuisance
of yourself if your project is not funded. Keep in mind that
often the competition is so keen, and the number of competitors so high, that your chances were slimmer than you
thought they were. For some publicly funded grant programs, there is a backlog of quality applications. Remember,
it's likely a different person or committee will read your
resubmittal. Twice in recent memory I've seen resubmittals
with nothing changed but the application date fully funded
on the second go-round.

SECTION THREE

Perform

"Civilization advances by extending the number of important operations which we can perform without thinking about them."

ALFRED NORTH WHITEHEAD

92

Get Together at the Get-Go

As soon as you win a grant:

1. Celebrate the good news with pizza, cake, champagne—or all three.
2. Because many months may have passed since you submitted your grant request, refresh the memories of all involved by circulating a brief summary of the project goals and objectives, activities, budget, and timelines. Depending on the complexity of the project, this could be merely a copy of the project abstract and the work plan, or a copy of the entire proposal.
3. Reassemble the cast of characters who will make the grant happen:
   - Staff who will directly carry out the grant activities
   - Staff with indirect roles, including administrative, accounting, and clerical staff
   - Other key people, such as staff of partnering agencies, subgrantees, or contracted agencies
4. At this meeting, the chair, typically the project director, leads a discussion that confirms:
   - The details in the notice or letter of grant award, including any unusual requirements
   - The project work plan, including roles and responsibilities in carrying out the grant (Special

attention should be given to any changes in the agency operating environment that have occurred since the grant was requested that impact project implementation.)

- Accountability for results, record keeping, and statistical reporting—including reports, reporting formats, and due dates

5. At the end of this meeting, the chair recaps who is responsible for what and when, and to whom (and how and when) they should report back. After this meeting, the chair follows up with a brief memo confirming roles and responsibilities.

93

Do, Document, Report . . . and Flourish

In general, grant compliance documentation and reporting is based on funders' efforts to avoid previous bad experiences with some grantees. In my opinion, about 10 to 15 percent of grantees cause most of the problems.

When you get the good news that you've been funded, and prior to the get together recommended in Strategy #92, revisit the funder's grant requirements. You'll find these requirements in the original grant guidelines; grants administration regulations referred to in the grant guidelines; the letter or notice of grant award, which may add special conditions; the contract, if one is presented by the funder; and documents on the funder's website.

It should be possible to identify the major recurring compliance and reporting issues for the types of grants you win; design your compliance system to address these issues. One way to do this is to attend training sessions and use any technical assistance resources offered by the funder. Typical compliance issues involve the following actions:

- Achieving the promised activity levels (utilization and productivity) within the timelines and with the staff and other resources in your grant request
- Meeting and documenting the cash or in-kind matching requirements of the grant during the correct time period
- Following proper procedures for procuring grant-funded services and materials, including subcontracting portions of the grant to other agencies or individuals
- Fulfilling the narrative, financial, and evaluation reporting requirements on a timely basis

For public funding, compliance requirements are likely to be substantial. Increasingly, grant compliance is documented and reported through online systems, especially for federal grants. State government grant funding may be based on deliverables-based contracts—you get reimbursed if and when your agency complies with the grant requirements (for example, by providing and documenting specific levels of service delivery). Larger funders, especially public ones, may split the roles of grant program officer and grant financial manager. Make sure you know which staff can make binding decisions for the funder and how you need to document changes to the scope or performance requirements of your grant. Private funding is likely to entail fewer documentation and reporting requirements. If, however, you develop your compliance system based on the most restrictive requirements, you will be better off in the long run.

Your agency may be selected for a performance review, which might entail funder staff visiting onsite and assessing the extent to which your agency is fulfilling its grant responsibilities. A performance review or grant audit is more likely if your agency has multiple grants from the same funder or larger grants (hundreds of thousands to millions of dollars). Protocols for these reviews or audits may be available at the funder's website—they can be a very useful tool in planning your compliance system at the outset of the grant. Here again, private funders are less likely to conduct performance reviews, but why would you want to incur the distrust of, say, a small foundation that might have been willing to fund your agency year after year?

If you do what you said you'd do with the grant money, document your compliance with grant requirements, and report timely and accurately on your activities, you will stay out of the doghouse as well as the big house.

94

Automate the Grantseeking and Grants Management Process

As you win and manage more and more grants, you will want to explore ways to improve your productivity and account-ability as you cope with increasing complexity. Numerous companies offer grantseeking and grants-management soft-ware, which you may want to consider buying. You can get a good idea of software functionality and costs by looking at sites such as Northern Lights Software, Oracle, and Dyna-Quest Technologies. There are many others. Due diligence is essential; talk to people who have used the software.

95

Married . . . with Funders

A long-term relationship with funders shares many of the attributes of a successful marriage, including mutual trust, concern for the other party's needs, and two-way communication.

If you accept funders as your partners, you will:

- Do what you promised with the money they granted you (or get their permission to change your plans)

- Show them how their support helps you achieve the objectives you share with them

If you do these two things, you will maintain a good reputation with funders.
They may even give you more money later.

96

Spend the Money

When you get a grant, spend the money as and when you promised you would. Sounds self-evident, but agencies with limited grants experience often fail to execute per their plan, seemingly regarding grant funding as more of an asset to be preserved than as a cash flow injection to do good things. I suspect they do this because they've had little experience handling large amounts of other people's money. (The first time I observed this phenomenon, I noticed that the grant was larger than the grantee's annual operating budget. No wonder they were having "digestive" problems.).

Funders want to know that you are ready to spend their money wisely and in a timely manner. Some funders will ask you to provide evidence of readiness to execute as part of your application, or condition the award on implementation within a 90- or 180-day timeline. They are simply putting you on notice that they want action and results in return for their money. As noted in Strategy #93, some funders will convert your grant award into a performance-based agreement, whereby you are reimbursed for documented activities and work products. In this scenario, you will need to finance activities until you are reimbursed. For equipment and construction/renovation projects, synchronicity of timing between expenditures and reimbursement are essential to your financial well-being and your working relationships with subcontractors or vendors.

Some grants are front-loaded, with additional funding in year one for equipment and other materials you will need throughout a multiyear grant period. Don't bank the money with the expectation that you can come back to the funder at the end of the project period and get their approval to buy hard assets with remaining funds earmarked for staff and services. They know this trick.

What if your operating situation has changed since you applied for the grant and you need to change your plan? You may be able to negotiate changes in objectives, activities, and timelines with the funder, but don't bet on it. Presumably, they gave you the money after comparing your proposed project with numerous others. If you make a practice of changing plans, you may get a reputation for unreliability—or worse, of leveraging money by lying about your agency's capabilities and intentions. Funders expect action and results.

97

Become a Grant Reviewer

Gain more insight into the funding process by serving as a grant reviewer. When you serve as a grant reviewer, you help funders pick the best proposals by reading, evaluating, and scoring competitive applications.

How do you become a grant reviewer? Look for invitations to become a reviewer on funder websites. Typically, the funding agency will want you to complete a brief application and email a copy of your resume. You'll need to demonstrate a combination of education, knowledge, and experience in your area of expertise.

Funders organize the review process and provide you and other reviewers with forms and instructions on how to evaluate competing applications. Reviews are conducted either in person at an office or hotel site, via teleconference, or via independent review, in which case you will review applications at your office and send your comments back to the funder. If travel is involved, the funder will probably pay your travel and related expenses and may pay you an honorarium. Sessions may last several days.

You're likely to meet interesting people as a grant reviewer. For example, the U.S. Public Health Service selects its review panels "to reflect diversity of ethnicity, gender, experience and geography." And later, when you are crafting your own proposals, you can think back to your grant review experience and imagine that group of reviewers and how they might critique your application.

98

Toot Your Own Horn (or Hire a Tooter)

It is well documented that, as media consumers, we place higher value on news than we do on paid advertising. Why not take advantage of credible, low-cost, grant-related publicity opportunities? Here are a few ideas:

- Announcement of your grant award (Be sure to coordinate your publicity with the funder.)
- Hiring of grant-funded staff
- Staff attendance at state, regional, national, or international meetings and training sessions
- Photo opportunities showing your project in action
- Local radio, TV, or newspaper interviews
- Presentations to business, civic, religious, and professional groups
- Inauguration of new grant-funded programs and facilities
- Other grant-funded special events and project milestones
- News articles that show your project is making a positive difference in people's lives

No "tooter" on your staff? Why not contract with a freelance writer who knows the right words and media? Wherever you are and however you do it, be sure to send a copy of news releases and subsequent coverage to the funder with a personal note, and be sure to follow their policies regarding mention of funder support.

99

Keep Track of Your Results

Keep track of your success rate with projects and funders by using a table like the one shown below.

Your Agency Grantseeking Track Record Time Period: _____						
#	Project Title	Funder	Submission Date	Response Date	Request Total	Funding Total

This table should be updated to keep you, your agency management, and your board informed of efforts and results; an annual summary report can help you gauge activity levels and results, and spot overall trends and outcomes. You can compute success rates for each type of funder (foundation, state and local government, federal government) and for all funders in the form of a percentage. For example, if you submitted five applications and three were funded, your success rate was 60 percent. You can also calculate a percentage success rate based on the dollars you requested, computed by dividing total dollars awarded by total dollars requested. Applications rejected on first submittal and funded on second submittal would be listed twice.

100

Winning from Losing

When you lose, try to find out why you lost, but don't make a career out of it.

Larger funders, especially public agencies, are more likely to provide you with written reviewers' comments. These comments may make you laugh, cry, gnash your teeth, or acknowledge ruefully that they were right.

Smaller, usually private funders may level with you on the phone, but they may not have the staffing, inclination, or time to explain their decision in writing. Ask what you can do differently next time around to merit their approval.

You may never find out the reason or reasons your proposal wasn't funded. It might merely have been fierce competition for a few awards. Sometimes it is who you know, but so what? Kvetching wastes energy and time you can devote to winning next time.

101

How to Keep Winning Grants

You can improve your grantseeking and grants-management results over time by continually strengthening your performance at each stage of the development process:

1. Prepare: Project planning, funding research, and organizational skills are paramount.
2. Persuade: Written and oral persuasive skills are most important.
3. Perform: Primarily project management skills.

Consider the following:

- Use the strategies in this book as a checklist against which to assess your performance and identify opportunities for improvement.
- If your agency uses Continuous Quality Improvement (CQI) or other means to conduct structural, process, and outcomes evaluation, use these methods to lend rigor to your grantseeking and grants-management assessment.
- If agency internal or self-assessment isn't working for you, gain insights and objectivity by swapping assessments with another local, noncompetitive agency or a similar agency in another community.

Evolution in the grantseeking and grants-management environment is certain to impact you and your agency over time. Funders' interests will change, as will perceptions of social, cultural, environmental and other problems, and the best solutions to these problems. You will probably get the very best results if you continue to adapt to change, accept responsibility for your own actions, and heed the maxim that "Practice is the best of all instructors."* Keep practicing.

---

*Publilius Syrus, 1st century B.C. writer.

INDEX

boilerplate file, 20–23
button-up checklist. *See* writing

case studies, 107
Catalog of Federal Domestic
    Assistance, 19, 75, 78
collaboration. *See* project design
Cooperating Collections
    (Foundation Center), 19,
    70, 74
Council on Foundations, 74

dissemination. *See* project design

earmarks, 32–34
editing. *See* writing
experts, involving, 23–24
evaluation. *See* project design
evidence of support and
    commitment, 118–119

FDSys, 79
Federal Register, 79
FOIA. *See* Freedom of
    Information Act
Foundation Center, 17, 18, 19,
    29, 70, 73, 74, 94
Foundation Directory Online,
    70, 72, 74
Freedom of Information Act,
    30–31
funding research, 25, 69–84,
    87–88
    assessing grant opportunities,
        87–88

company-sponsored
    foundations, 72–73
community foundations,
    74–75
contacting funders, 81–82
corporate giving programs,
    73–74
federal funding, 77–80
grant opportunities
    workshops, 83–84
independent private
    foundations, 71–72
local funding, 75–76
overview, 69–70
researching potential
    funders, 25
state funding, 76–77
Web postings, 80

goals, defining, 47
grant application guidelines,
    89–90
    analysis of, 89
    clarifications of, 90
grant reviewer, serving as a, 136
grants, 3–12, 18–19, 28–32,
    35–40, 117–118
    analyzing abstracts of
        previously funded
        projects, 31–32
    basis for all successful
        grantseeking, 3
    benefits of, 8
    bookshelf (references), 18–19
    definition, 5
    grantseeker's sweet spot, 6–7

grantseeking, alternative
methods of, 35–40
obtaining copies of funded
grant projects, 30–31
prudent buyer concept, and,
117–118
readiness to seek, assessment
of, 9–12
seven deadly grantseeking
sins, 28–29
grants consultants, assessing and
using, 36–38
grants development, 13–15,
26–28
assigning responsibility for,
13–14
board of directors
involvement in, 15
management approval
for, 14
plan contents, 26–28
grants.gov, 78, 80
grants management, 129–135,
137–141
compliance and reporting,
130–132
continually improving results,
140–141
execution, 134–135
getting organized upon notice
of grant award, 129–130
grantor-grantee relationship,
133–134
grantseeking track record,
138–139
performance reviews
(grant audits), 132
publicity, 137–138

software (automating the
grantseeking and grants
management process),
133

learning curve, climbing the
grantseeker's, 17
letter of inquiry, 94

multiple submissions, 122–123

naming of grant projects, 41–42

objectives, defining, 47
one-pager, 92–93
outline, 92–93
purpose and audience, 92
Open Records acts, 31

pilot test, 69
project design, 42–68, 82, 97–99
alternatives to grants,
consideration of, 49–50
based on funders' needs,
98–99
based on funding criteria, 82
budgeting, 60, 97–98
collaboration, 55–57
cost-sharing (matching),
61–62
dissemination, 66–67
evaluation, 64–66
planning, the importance of,
42–43
planning for impediments,
57–58
planning process, completion
of, 68
problem description, 45–46

replicating a successful
    project, 51
"sight" (site) visit, 52–55
solution description, 47–48
sustainability, 62–63
team, 43–45
work plan, 59–60
proposal, format and contents,
    95–96

responses to failure
    (reapplication and other),
    125–126, 139

site visit (funder's), 124–125
strategies (definition), 47
sustainability. *See* project design
SWOT analysis, 11–12, 27

tracking tool, 91

work plan. *See* project design
writing, 96–97, 99–122
    abstract, 96–97
    answering the funder's
        questions, 107–108
    button-up checklist, 120–121
    coping strategies, 99–101
    editing, 111–113, 116
    specialized terminology, use
        of, 114
    specificity, the importance
        of, 102
    visual presentation, 115
    writer's block (combatting),
        105–106
    writing process, 104–105

Books from Allworth Press

Allworth Press is an imprint of Skyhorse Publishing, Inc. Selected titles are listed below.

Guide to Getting Arts Grants
by Ellen Liberatori (6 x 9, 272 pages, paperback, $19.95)

Branding for Nonprofits
by DK Holland (6 x 9, 208 pages, paperback, $19.95)

Emotional Branding: The New Paradigm for Connecting Brands to People, Updated and Revised Edition
by Marc Gobe (6 x 9, 353 pages, paperback, $19.95)

Performing Arts Management: A Handbook of Professional Practices
by Tobie S. Stein (8 ½ x 11, 552 pages, paperback, $50.00)

Brand Thinking and Other Noble Pursuits
by Debbie Millman (6 x 9, 256 pages, hardcover, $29.95)

The Smart Consumer's Guide to Good Credit: An Expert's Guide to All the Tools You Need to Get Good Credit in a Bad Economy
by John Ulzheimer (5 ½ x 8 ¼, 256 pages, paperback, $14.95)

Legal Guide for the Visual Artist, Fifth Edition
by Tad Crawford (8 ½ x 11, 304 pages, paperback, $29.95)

Fine Art Publicity: The Complete Guide for Galleries and Artists
by Susan Abbott (6 x 9, 192 pages, paperback, $19.95)

Building the Successful Theater Company
by Lisa Mulcahy (6 x 9, 240 pages, paperback, $19.95)

Promote Your Book: Over 250 Proven, Low-Cost Tips and Techniques for the Enterprising Author
by Patricia Fry (5 ½ x 8 ¼, 224 pages, paperback, $19.95)

To see our complete catalog or to order online, please visit *www.allworth.com*.